Piano/Vocal/Chords

80 YEARS OF POPULAR MUSIC

THE EIGHTIES

Project Manager: CAROL CUELLAR
Copy Editors: NADINE DEMARCO & DONNA SALZBURG
Cover Design: HEADLINE PUBLICITY LIMITED
Book Art Layout: LISA GREENE MANE
Text Research: CAROL CUELLAR & DAVID C. OLSEN

1980

U.S. President Jimmy Carter told the Senate it should not ratify the SALT nuclear arms treaty with the USSR until the Soviets withdrew from Afghanistan. Top TV shows were "Dallas" (seen by more U.S. viewers than any other TV program), "60 Minutes," and "Dukes of Hazzard." Top grossing films of the year were *Airplane, Any Which Way You Can, The Empire Strikes Back, 9 to 5*, and *Stir Crazy*. It was a sad day for John Lennon fans around the world as news broke about his murder outside his New York apartment. Michael Jackson was awarded his first Grammy for *Thriller*. At least 15 people were killed when long dormant volcano Mt. St. Helens in Washington State erupted. Ronald Reagan was elected the fortieth U.S. President.

1981

John W. Hinckley Jr. shot President Reagan. He survived after two hours of surgery for a wound in his left lung. *Arthur* and *Superman II* were two of the top grossing films of the year. IBM introduced the personal computer. Prince Charles, British heir to the throne, tied the knot with Lady Diana Spencer. It was the wedding of the decade as millions around the world watched on TV and happy crowds lined the streets of London.

1982

The first successful artificial heart transplant was completed. The largest cash robbery in U.S. history made news when thieves made off with $9.8 million in New York City. Top grossing films were *E.T., An Officer and a Gentleman*, and *Rocky III*. There was war in the Falkland Islands when the Argentine military government invaded. Three days later, British troops retook the land. Princess Grace of Monaco was killed when her car went off a mountain road and fell 12 feet.

1983

This was the year of the Cabbage Patch doll, as parents rushed to fill their children's wish lists, only to find the shelves empty. The supply was nowhere near the demand. Baseball was the top spectator sport, drawing 78,051,343 fans and dropping horse racing to second place. President Reagan designated a federal holiday honoring Dr. Martin Luther King, Jr., for the third Monday of January. Bon Jovi signed to Mercury Records.

1984

After a violent argument, Reverend Marvin Gaye shot and killed his son Marvin Gaye. Ronald Reagan was re-elected President of the United States in the greatest Republican landslide in history. The first heart and liver transplant was performed on a six-year-old Texas girl. Identification of a virus thought to cause acquired immune deficiency syndrome (AIDS) was announced by federal researchers. "Dynasty" was the number one TV program, and *Beverly Hills Cop, Ghostbusters*, and *Indiana Jones and the Temple of Doom* were the top grossing films. *Thriller* by Michael Jackson was the top selling album.

1985

The Titanic luxury liner was finally discovered by a U.S.-French exploration team. Sixty million dollars was raised when Bob Geldof organized LiveAid. The idea came after the huge success of "Do They Know It's Christmas," which was recorded for the benefit of the famine victims in Ethiopia. The number one TV show was "The Cosby Show." *Back to the Future, The Color Purple*, and *Rocky IV* were the top grossing films. American rock and country singer Rick Nelson was killed, along with his fiancée and four band members, when a chartered DC3 carrying them between concerts in Guntersville, Alabama, and Dallas, Texas, caught fire and crashed.

1986

Christina McAuliffe, an ordinary citizen and school teacher was chosen to be a part of the U.S. space shuttle Challenger team. Challenger exploded in a ball of fire soon after blasting off for its tenth flight, killing all seven aboard instantly. Mike Tyson became boxing's youngest heavyweight champion in the world at the age of 20 after winning the fight against Trevor Berbick.

1987

The British voted in for a third term Margaret Thatcher as Prime Minister of the U.K. Hollywood lost one of its great legends, Fred Astaire, at the age of 88. The Federal government approved the drug AZT. Although not a cure for AIDS, tests showed that it could extend the life of the patient. Top grossing films were *Beverly Hills Cop 2, Fatal Attraction*, and *Good Morning Vietnam*.

1988

The writers of American soap operas went on strike for improved terms, and there were fears that "Dynasty" and "Dallas" would be threatened. An American jumbo jet exploded over the Scottish town of Locherbie, killing 270 people aboard and 11 on the ground. George Bush won the Presidential election. American rock 'n' roll singer/songwriter Roy Orbison died of a heart attack at the age of 52. More than 100,000 people were killed when an enormous earthquake hit Armenia.

1989

American heavyweight boxer Mike Tyson defeated British champion Frank Bruno. November 10, the sound of church bells, hooting horns, and thousands of cheering people celebrated the fall of the Berlin Wall. Berliners east and west mingled freely and looked forward to a new reunited Germany. Box office blockbuster *Batman* was the biggest movie of the year. American troops invaded Panama, ousted dictator Manuel Noriega, and installed a new government led by Guillermo Endara.

CONTENTS

Song	Artist	Page
AFRICA	TOTO	10
AFTER ALL (LOVE THEME FROM *CHANCES ARE*)	CHER & PETER CETERA	5
AGAINST ALL ODDS (TAKE A LOOK AT ME NOW)	PHIL COLLINS	16
AGAINST THE WIND	BOB SEGER & THE SILVER BULLET BAND	19
ALL AT ONCE	WHITNEY HOUSTON	24
ALL NIGHT LONG	LIONEL RICHIE	28
ANYTHING FOR YOU	GLORIA ESTEFAN & THE MIAMI SOUND MACHINE	36
ARTHUR'S THEME (BEST THAT YOU CAN DO)	CHRISTOPHER CROSS	46
BABY, COME TO ME	PATTI AUSTIN & JAMES INGRAM	41
BACK IN THE HIGH LIFE AGAIN	STEVE WINWOOD	50
CUTS LIKE A KNIFE	BRYAN ADAMS	55
DON'T MEAN NOTHING	RICHARD MARX	62
DON'T RUSH ME	TAYLOR DAYNE	67
DON'T YOU KNOW WHAT THE NIGHT CAN DO	STEVE WINWOOD	74
EASY LOVER	PHIL COLLINS	70
ENDLESS SUMMER NIGHTS	RICHARD MARX	79
FAITHFULLY	JOURNEY	84
FOREVER	KENNY LOGGINS	88
FOREVER I DO (THE WEDDING SONG)	LOU RAWLS	94
FROM A DISTANCE	BETTE MIDLER	100
HEAVEN	BRYAN ADAMS	104
HELLO	LIONEL RICHIE	97
HOLD ON TO THE NIGHTS	RICHARD MARX	108
HOW WILL I KNOW	WHITNEY HOUSTON	114
I KNEW YOU WERE WAITING (FOR ME)	ARETHA FRANKLIN & GEORGE MICHAEL	118
I WANNA DANCE WITH SOMEBODY (WHO LOVES ME)	WHITNEY HOUSTON	136
I WILL ALWAYS LOVE YOU	DOLLY PARTON	122
IF EVER YOU'RE IN MY ARMS AGAIN	PEABO BRYSON	124
IN THE AIR TONIGHT	PHIL COLLINS	130
KEY LARGO	BERTIE HIGGINS	139
THE LADY IN RED	CHRIS DEBURGH	148
LIKE A ROCK	BOB SEGER & THE SILVER BULLET BAND	152
THE LIVING YEARS	MIKE & THE MECHANICS	172
LOVE CHANGES (EVERYTHING)	CLIMIE FISHER	176
MAN IN THE MIRROR	MICHAEL JACKSON	159
MANEATER	HALL AND OATES	180
MY LOVE	LIONEL RICHIE	186
ON THE WINGS OF LOVE	JEFFREY OSBORNE	192
ONE IN A MILLION YOU	LARRY GRAHAM	183
ONE MORE NIGHT	PHIL COLLINS	198
OPEN ARMS	JOURNEY	204
SAY YOU, SAY ME	LIONEL RICHIE	207
SHOULD'VE KNOWN BETTER	RICHARD MARX	212
SHOW ME THE WAY	STYX	144
SUDDENLY	OLIVIA NEWTON-JOHN & CLIFF RICHARD	219
TAKE ME HOME	PHIL COLLINS	222
(I'VE HAD) THE TIME OF MY LIFE	BILL MEDLEY & JENNIFER WARNES	228
TONIGHT I CELEBRATE MY LOVE	PEABO BRYSON & ROBERTA FLACK	232
TRULY	LIONEL RICHIE	244
UP WHERE WE BELONG	JOE COCKER	236
WAITING FOR A STAR TO FALL	BOY MEETS GIRL	240
WHAT'S LOVE GOT TO DO WITH IT	TINA TURNER	252
WHILE YOU SEE A CHANCE	STEVE WINWOOD	247
WORDS GET IN THE WAY	GLORIA ESTEFAN	264
YOU ARE	LIONEL RICHIE	258

From the Tri-Star Pictures Film "CHANCES ARE"

AFTER ALL

(Love Theme from "Chances Are")

Words and Music by
DEAN PITCHFORD and
TOM SNOW

B
She:
E/G♯
A(9)
straight.
I still re-mem - ber when

C♯m7
F♯m
E/G♯
your kiss was so brand new.
Ev-ery mem-o-ry re-peats, ev-ery

A
E/G♯
Both:
A
B
A/B B
step I take re-treats.
Ev-ery jour-ney al - ways brings me back to you.
Af-ter
cresc.

Chorus:
E
C♯m
all the stops and starts, we keep com-in' back to these two hearts, two
f

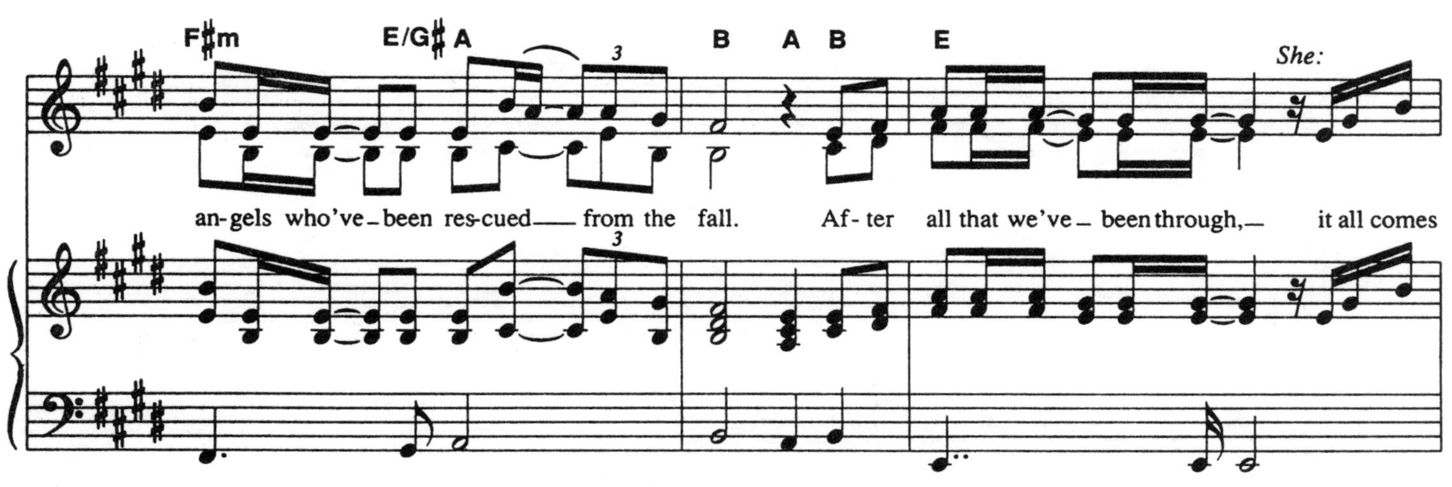
F♯m
E/G♯
A
B
A
B
E
She:
an-gels who've been res-cued from the fall. Af-ter all that we've been through, it all comes

G♯m7
G♯/B♯
C♯m
Both:
A
He:
down to me and you. I guess it's meant to be, for

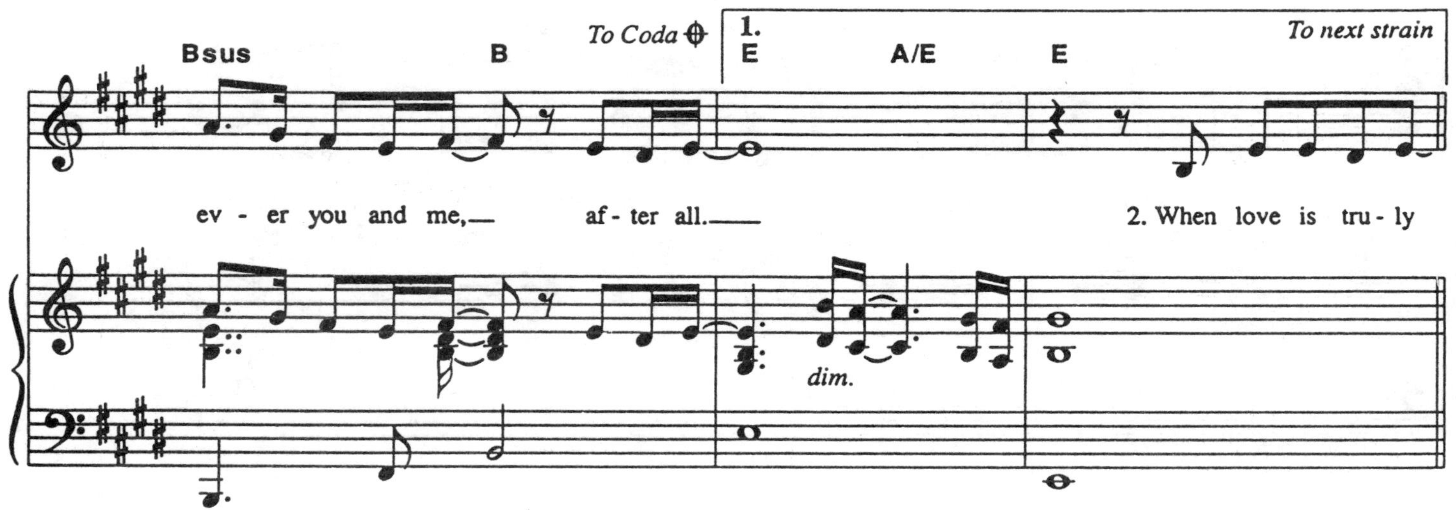

To Coda
1.
To next strain
Bsus
B
E
A/E
E
ev - er you and me,
af - ter all.
2. When love is tru - ly
dim.

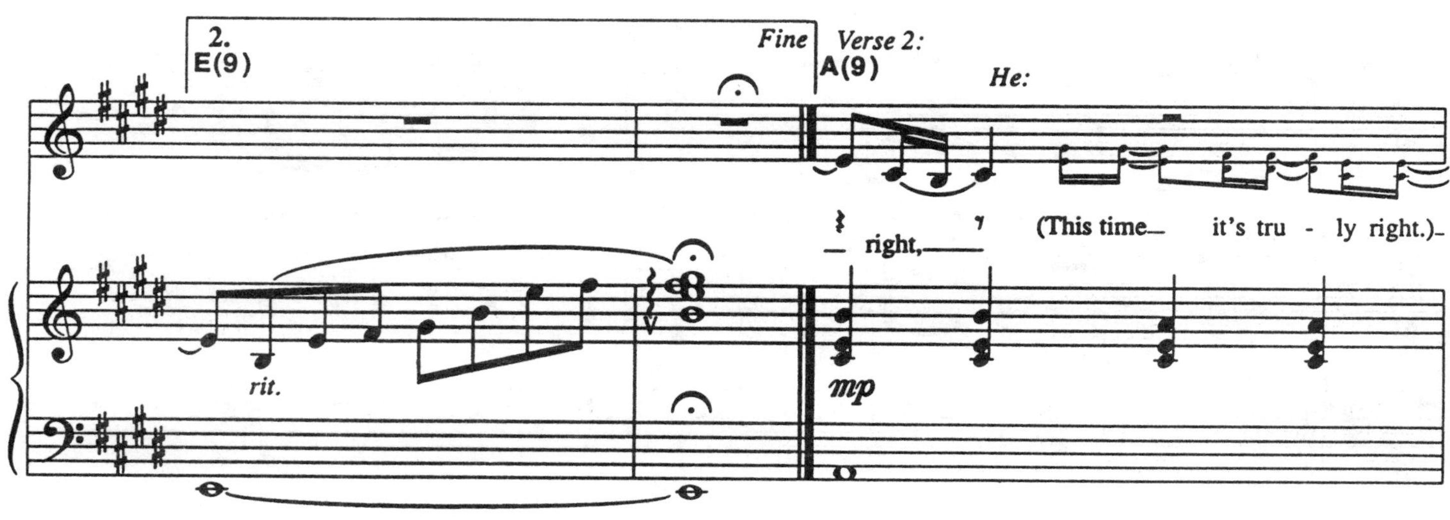

2.
Fine
Verse 2:
E(9)
A(9)
He:
right,
(This time it's tru - ly right.)
rit.
mp

She:
E(9)
C♯m7
Both:
E/G♯
A
it lives from year to year.
It chang - es as it

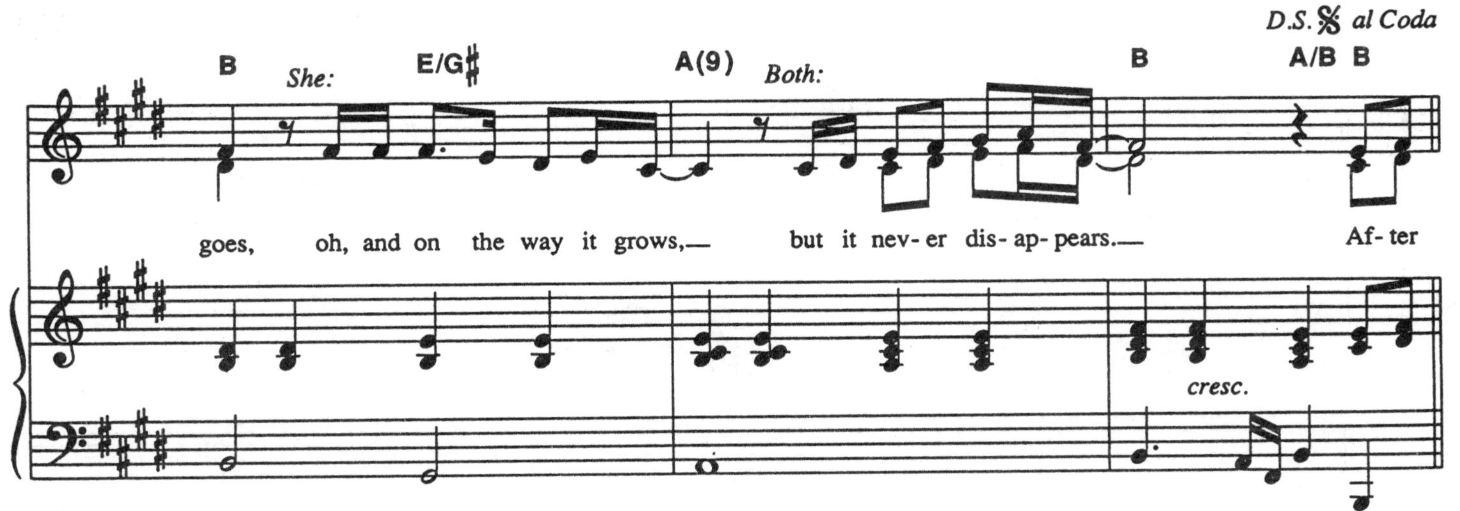
D.S. 𝄋 al Coda
B
She:
E/G♯
A(9)
Both:
B
A/B B
goes, oh, and on the way it grows,— but it nev-er dis-ap-pears.— Af-ter
cresc.

Coda
E
Esus
(Bridge:)
Asus
Al - ways just be - yond— my touch,—

D.S. 𝄋 al Fine
G♯/B♯
C♯m
A
B
You know I need-ed you— so much. Af-ter all, what else is liv-in' for?— Af-ter

AFRICA

Words and Music by
DAVID PAICH and JEFF PORCARO

D♯m7 G♯m7 B/F♯ A/E

ech - o - in' to - night.__ She hears on - ly whis - pers of some

E/F♯ Emaj7/G♯ A G♯m C♯m7

qui - et con - ver - sa - tion.

B D♯m7 G♯m7

She's com - ing in, twelve thir - ty flight.__
The wild dogs cry out in the night,__ as

B/F♯ A/E E/F♯

Moon - lit wings__ re - flect the stars__ that guide me toward__ sal -
they grow rest - less, long - ing for__ some sol - i - tar - y

Emaj7/G♯ A G♯m C♯m7 4 fr. 4 fr.

va - tion.
com - pa - ny.

B D♯m7 6 fr. G♯m7 4 fr.

I stopped an old man a - long the way,
I know that I must do what's right, sure as

B/F♯ A/E E/F♯

hop - ing to find some old for - got - ten words or an - cient
Kil - i - man - ja - ro ris - es like O - lym - pus a - bove the

Emaj7/G♯ A G♯m C♯m7 4 fr. 4 fr.

mel - o - dies.
Se - ren - ge - ti.

B
D♯m7
6 fr.
G♯m7
4 fr.
He turned to me as if to say,
I seem to cure what's deep - in - side,
A
G♯m
C♯m7
4 fr.
"Hur - ry, boy, it's wait - ing there for you."
fright - ened of this thing that I've be - come.
F♯m
It's gon - na take a lot
D
A
E
to drag me a - way from you.

F#m
D
A
There's noth - ing that a hun - dred men __ or more __ could ev - er do. __
E
F#m
D
__ I bless the rains __ down in Af -
A
E
F#m
ri - ca. __ Gon - na take some time __
D
A
C#m7
4 fr.
E
__ to do __ the things we nev - er had. __

F♯m
E/G♯
A
G♯m
C♯m7
4 fr.
Repeat and fade

From the Columbia Pictures Film "AGAINST ALL ODDS"

AGAINST ALL ODDS
(Take a Look at Me Now)

Words and Music by
PHIL COLLINS

Against All Odds - 3 - 1

Db/Ab
Eb7/Ab
well, there's just an emp-ty space. And there's noth - ing
mf
Bbm7
Gb
Ebm7
Absus
left here to re-mind me, just the mem - 'ry of your face. Well, take a look at me now.
Db/Ab
Eb7/Ab
1. well there's just an empty space. And you com - in' back
2. 'cause there's just an emp-ty space. But to wait
3. 'cause I'll still be stand-ing here. And you com - in' back
Bbm7
Gb
1.
Ebm7
to me is a-gainst the odds, and that's what I've got to face.
for you is all I can do, and that's what
to me is a-gainst all odds, it's the chance

Verse 2:
How can you just walk away from me,
When all I can do is watch you leave?
'Cause we shared the laughter and the pain,
And even shared the tears.
You're the only one who really knew me at all.
(To Chorus:)

Verse 3:
I wish I could just make you turn around,
Turn around and see me cry,
There's so much I need to say to you,
So many reasons why.
You're the only one who really knew me at all.
(To Chorus:)

AGAINST THE WIND

Words and Music by
BOB SEGER

Medium Rock beat
G
G
It seems like yes - ter - day,
And the years rolled slow - ly past.
Instrumental
Bm
but it was long a - go.
And I found my - self a - lone,

C
G
Ja - ney was love - ly. She was the queen of my nights,
sur-round-ed by stran - gers I thought were my friends.
D
C
there in the dark - ness with the ra - di - o play-in' low, and
I found my-self fur-ther and fur - ther from my home, and
G
the se - crets that we shared,
I guess I lost my way.
Bm
the moun - tains that we moved,
There were oh so man - y roads.
I was
3

C G

caught like a wild fire out of con - trol ___ till there was
liv - in' to run and run - nin' to live. ___ Nev - er

C D

noth - in' left ___ to burn ___ and noth - in' left to prove. ___
wor - ried a - bout pay - in', ___ or e - ven how much I owed. ___

Em D

And I re - mem - ber what she ___ said to
Mov - in' eight miles a min - ute for months at a
Well, those drift - er's days are ___ past me

G Em C

me, ___ how she swore ___ that it nev - er would end. ___
time, ___ break - in' all ___ of the rules ___ that would bend, ___
now. ___ I've got so ___ much more to ___ think a - bout: ___

G
Em
D
I re - mem-ber how she held me oh so
I be - gan to find my - self
dead - lines and com -
C
tight.
search-in',
mit- ments,
Wish I did-n't know now what I did-n't know
search-in' for shel - ter a - gain and a -
what to leave in, what to leave
D
G
Bm
then.
gain.
out.
A-gainst the wind,
A-gainst the wind,
A-gainst the wind,
C
G
we were run-nin' a - gainst the wind.
lit - tle some-thin' a - gainst the wind.
I'm still run - nin' a - gainst the wind.
We were
I
I'm

C
Bm
Am
C
G
To Coda
young and strong. We were run-nin' a-gainst the wind.
found my-self seek-in' shel-ter a-gainst the wind.
old-er now, but still run-nin' a-gainst the wind.
1.
2.
D. S. al Coda
Coda
C
Bm
D
Well, I'm old-er now, and still run-nin' a-gainst the
Repeat and fade
C
G
wind, a-gainst the wind. A-gainst the

ALL AT ONCE

Words by
JEFFREY OSBORNE and MICHAEL MASSER

Music by
MICHAEL MASSER

Dm7 Gm7 Cm7 E♭/F F7
you're not com - ing back. And it fi - n'lly hit me all at once.
B♭ E♭/B♭ B♭ F/A
All at once I
Gm B♭/F E♭ F/E♭
start - ed count - ing tear - drops and at least a mil - lion fell. My
Dm7 Gm7 Cm7 E♭/F
eyes be-gan to swell, and all my dreams were shat - tered all at once.
Bridge:
B♭ E♭ B♭/D D7-9 D/F♯ Gm F
Ev - er since I met you, you're the on - ly love I've known,
mf

Eb
Bb/D
Gm7
Cm7
and I can't for - get you, though I must face it all a -
Cm7/F
Gb/Ab
Ab7
Chorus:
Db
Fm7/Bb
Bb/D
lone. All at once I'm drift - ing on a lone -
cresc.
f
Ebm7
Ab
Ab/Gb
Fm7
Bbm7
- ly sea, wish - ing you'd come back to me. And that's all that mat -
Gbmaj9
Gb/Ab
Db
Fm7/Bb
Bb/D
- ters now. All at once I'm drift - ing on a lone -
Ebm7
Ab
Ab/Gb
Fm7
Bbm7
- ly sea, hold - ing on to mem - o-ries. And it hurts me more

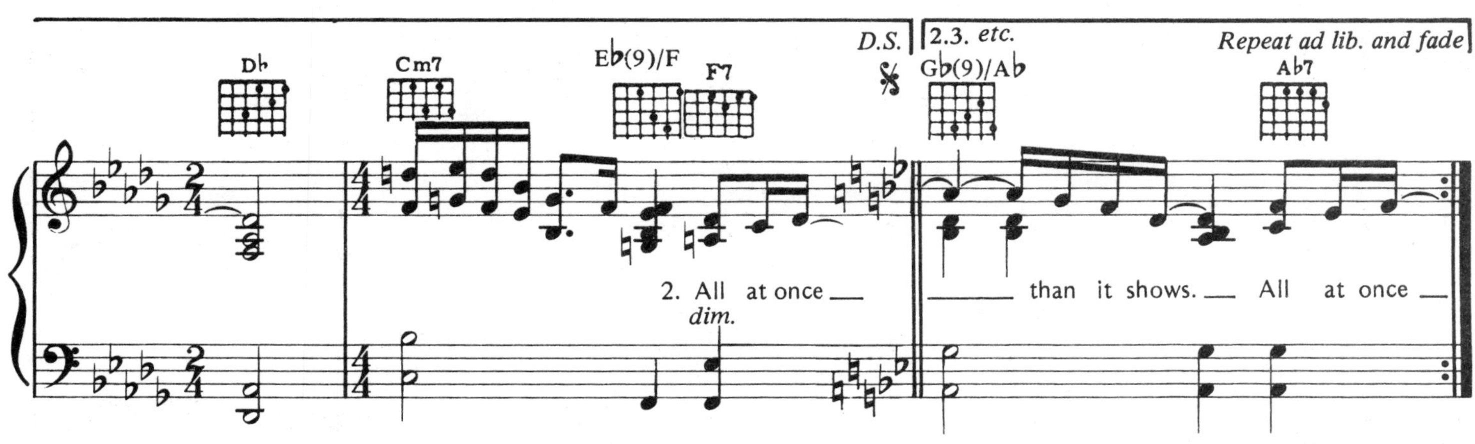

Verse 2:
All at once
I looked around and found
That you were with another love,
In someone else's arms,
And all my dreams were shattered
All at once.
All at once
The smile that used to greet me
Brightens someone else's day.
She took your smile away,
And left me with just mem'ries
All at once.
(To Bridge:)

ALL NIGHT LONG (ALL NIGHT)

Words and Music by
LIONEL RICHIE

Moderate Caribbean feel (♩ = about 104)

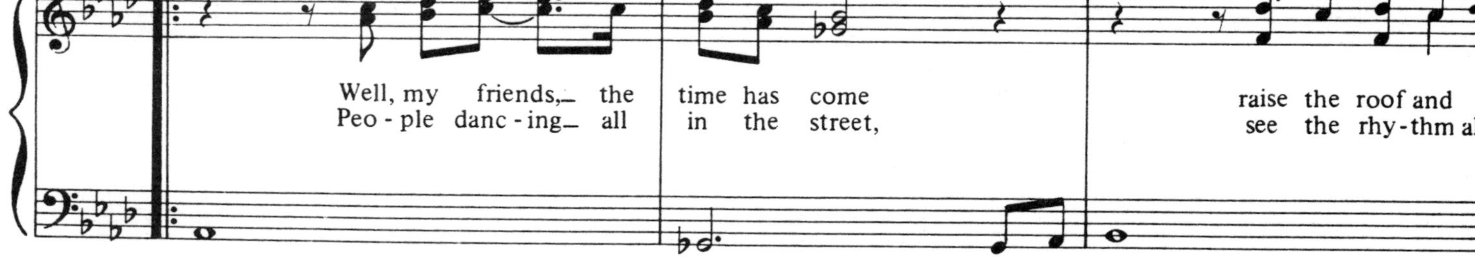

G
Ab
F
Gb
have some fun.
in their feet.
Throw a - way the
Life is good.
work to be done.
wild, and sweet.
Am
5fr.
Bbm
G
Ab
let the mu - sic
let the mu - sic
play on (play on, play on).
play on (play on, play on).
F
Gb
Am
5fr.
Bbm
Ev - 'ry - bod - y sing,
Feel it in your heart
ev - 'ry - bod - y dance,
and feel it in your soul,
lose your - self in
let the mu - sic
G
Ab
F
Gb
wild ro - mance. We're going to
take con - trol. We're going to
par - ti' ka - ra - mu,
par - ti' lim - ing,
fi - es - ta, for - ev - er.
fi - es - ta, for - ev - er.

2nd time omit these bars

Am 5fr. Bbm — *G* Ab

Come on — and sing a - long: — We're going — to par - ty, ka - ra - mu,
Come on — and

F Gb — *Am* 5fr. Bbm — *G* Ab

fi - es - ta, for - ev - er. Come on — and sing — a - long: —
sing — my — song: —

Chorus

G Ab — *F* Gb

All night — long, — (All night —) all night, — All night

G Ab — *F* Gb

long, — (All night —) all night, — All night — long, — all night, —

1. G
A♭
All night
long,
Oh.
2. G
A♭
(All night_)
long,
(All night_)
Yeah!
N.C.
F
G♭
Once you_get start - ed_ you can't sit_down,
N.C.
F
G♭
Come join_the fun, it's_ a mer - ry - go - round,

F
N.C.
Gb
Ev - 'ry - one's danc - ing their trou - bles a - way,
Fmaj7
Em7
Fmaj7
Em7
N.C.
Gbmaj7
Fm7
Gbmaj7
Fm7
Come join our par - ty, see how we play!
Fmaj7
Em7
Fmaj7
Em7
N.C.
Gbmaj7 Fm7
Gbmaj7
Fm7
N.C.
N.C.
Tom bo li de say de moi ya
Yeah, Jam - bo Jum - bo

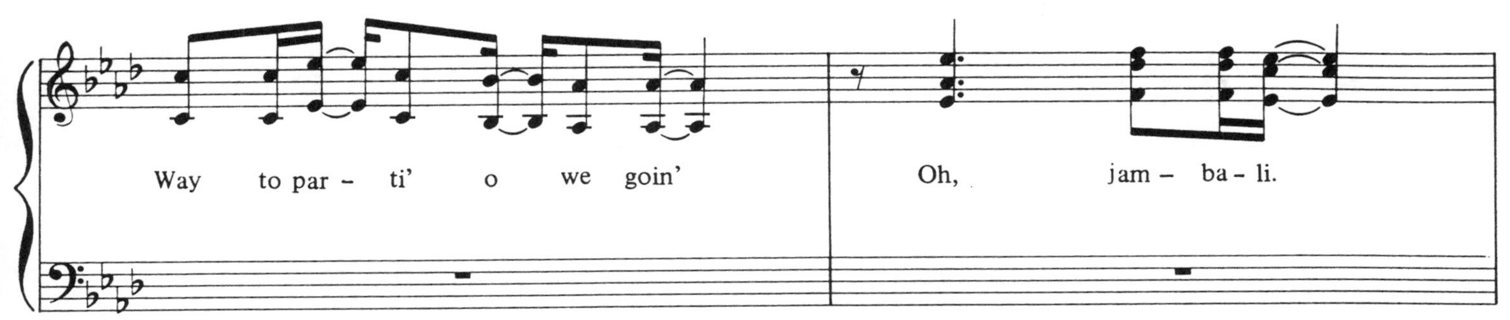

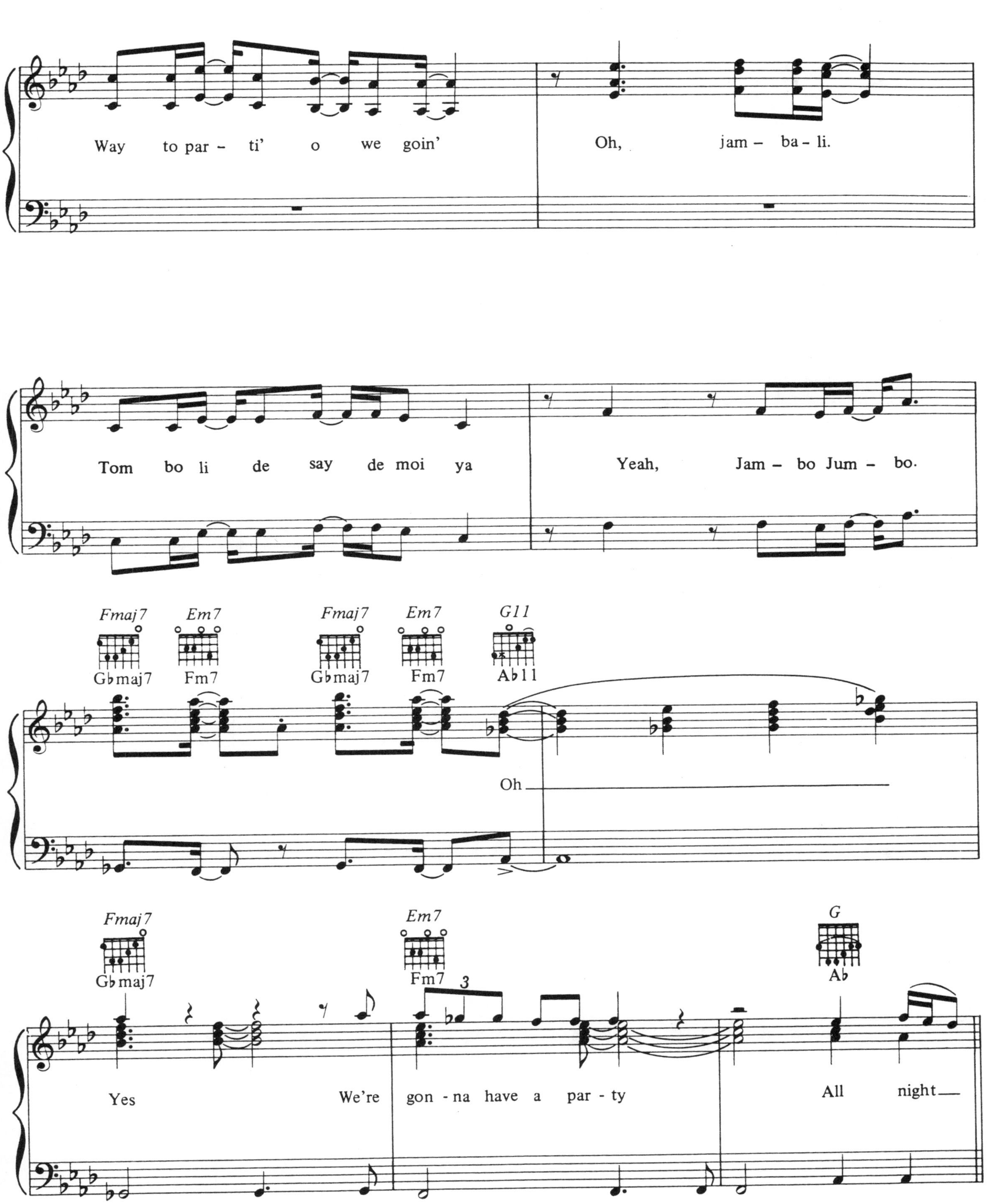

Way to par – ti' o we goin'
Oh, jam – ba – li.
Tom bo li de say de moi ya
Yeah, Jam – bo Jum – bo.
Fmaj7
Em7
Fmaj7
Em7
G11
G♭maj7
Fm7
G♭maj7
Fm7
A♭11
Oh
Fmaj7
Em7
G
G♭maj7
Fm7
A♭
3
Yes We're gon - na have a par - ty All night

F
Gb
long, (All night) all night, All night
G
Ab
long, (All night) all night, All night
F
Gb
long, all night, All night
G
Ab
long (All night) (All night)

F
G♭
Ev - 'ry - one you meet,
they're
jam - ming in the street,
All night
G
A♭
long.
(All night)
(All night)
F
G♭
G
A♭
Repeat and fade
(All night)
(All night)

ANYTHING FOR YOU

Words and Music by
GLORIA ESTEFAN

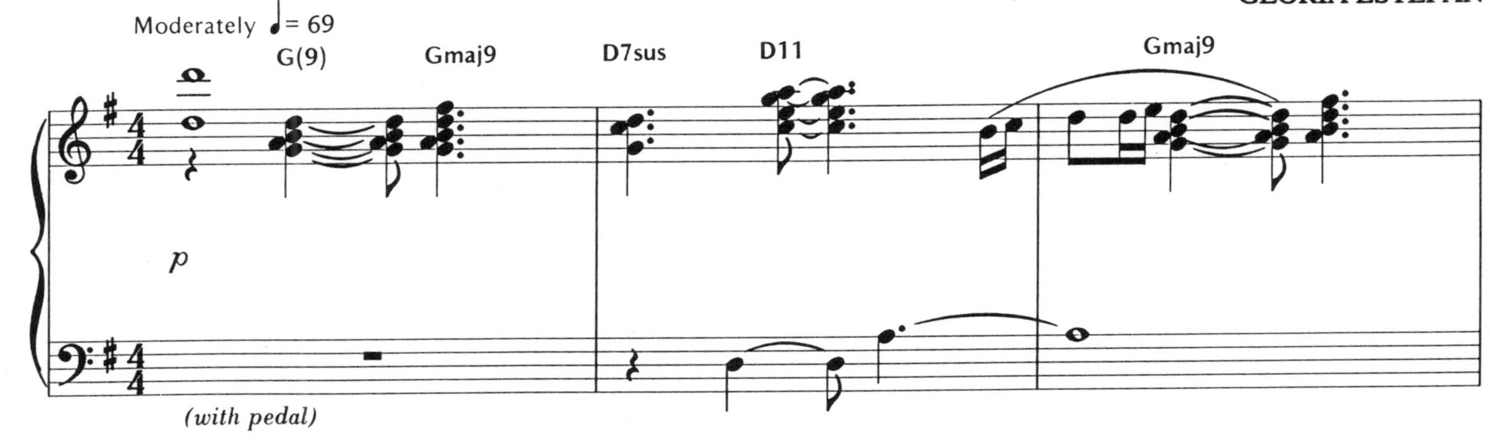

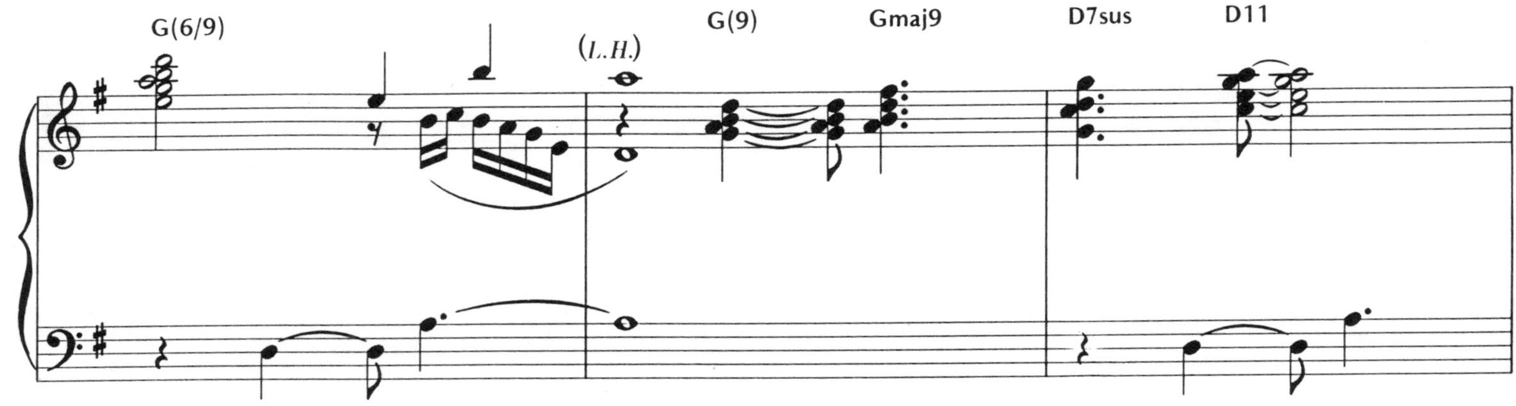

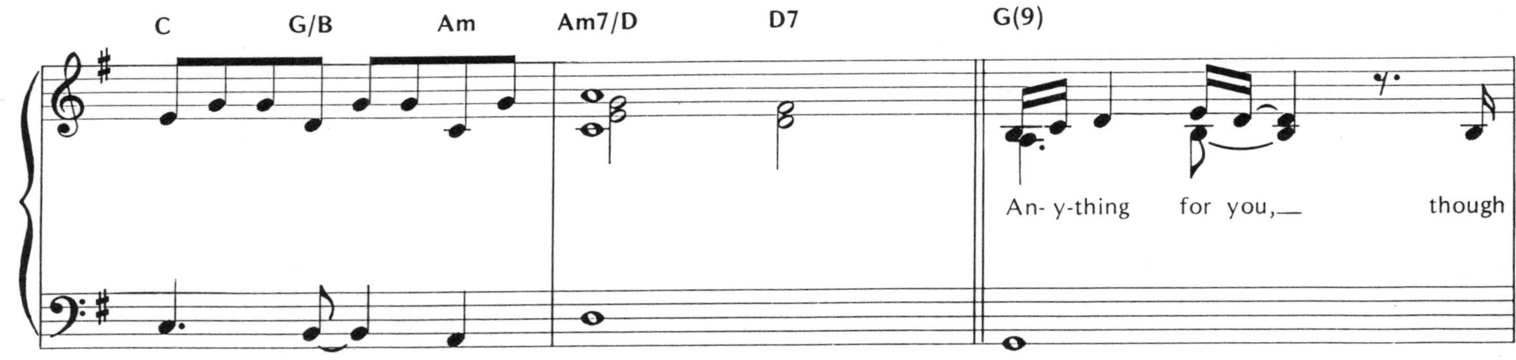

Cmaj9
G/D
drag - ging on — and on, — and for -
ev - er's been — and gone. — Still, I can't
Em7
C(9)
Dsus
D
fig - ure what — went wrong. —
I'd still do
G(9)
D7sus
D
G(9)
D/E
Em7
an - y-thing for you; — I'll
play your game. — You
hurt me through and through, but you can
Dm9
G7sus
G7
Cmaj9
have your way. — I can pre
- tend each time — I see — you that I don't
G/D
(D2/G)
G/D
Em7
A7
care and I don't need — you. And though you'll
nev - er see — me cry - ing; you know, in-

C/D
D
C/D
D
G(9)
side I feel like dy - ing.
And I'd do
an - y-thing for you,
in-
Dsus
D
G/B
G/A
G
spite of it all.
I've
learned so much from you;
you
cresc.
Dm7/F
G/A
C/D
made me strong.
Don't you ev - er
think that I don't love you, that for one
mf
G/D
C/D
min - ute I for - got you.
But some-times
things don't work out right,
and you just
Dm9
Dm9/A
F/G
G7/B
Cmaj7
have to say good-bye.
I hope you
find some-one to please you, some-one who'll
cresc.
f

G/D
G/B
G
Em7
care, and nev-er leave you. But if that some-one ev - er hurts you, you just might
dim.
Dsus7
D7
need a friend to turn to. And I'd do
p
G(9)
Dsus7
D
an - y-thing for you; I'll give you up, if
G
D/E
Em7
Dm7
G7sus
G
that's what I should do to make you hap - py. I can pre -
cresc.
Cmaj9
G/D
tend each time I see you that I don't care and I don't need you. And though in-
mf

Em7 G/A Dm7 Dm/A G7sus G7/B
side I feel like dy - ing, you know you'll nev - er see me cry - ing. Don't you ev - er
Cmaj9 G/D
think that I don't love you, that for one min - ute I for-got you. But some-times
Em7 G/A Dm9 Dm9/A G7sus G7/B
things don't work our right, and you just have to say good - bye.
Cmaj7 G/D
Instrumental Solo.
Repeat ad lib. and fade
Em7 Em7/A Dm7 Dm7/A G7/B

BABY, COME TO ME

Words and Music by
ROD TEMPERTON

Moderately
Am7
Dm7
Em7
mp
Am
D/A
Am7
F/G
G
1.Think - in' back in time, when love was
2.(See additional lyrics)
on - ly in the mind, I re - a - lize

F/G G Am7 D/A Am7 D/A
ain't no sec-ond chance; you've got to hold on to ro-mance. Don't
F/G G F/G G Am7
let it slide. There's a
B♭maj7 Am7
spe - cial kind of mag - ic in the air when you
A♭maj7 G11 F/G G
find an - oth-er heart that needs to share. Ba - by,
cresc.

Chorus:
Cm7
Fm9
Ab/Bb
Fm
come to me; let me put my arms a-round you. This was
(you.)
mf
Gm7
Ebmaj9
G7-9
meant to be, and I'm oh, so glad I found you. Need you
Cm7
Fm9
Ab/Bb
Fm
ev - 'ry day; got to have your love a-round me. Ba - by,
Gm7
To Coda
1.
Dm7
G7-9
al - ways stay, 'cause I can't go back to liv - in' with-out

D.S. al Coda
2.3. etc.
D.S.S. al Chorus repeat and fade
Cm
Cm/B♭
B♭
Dm7
G7-9
you.
can't go back to liv - in' with-out
descresc.
Coda
Dm7
G7-9
Csus
can't go back to liv - in' with-out you.
C
A♭maj7
The night can get
Cm7
A♭/B♭
cold; there's a chill to ev-'ry eve - ning

2. Spendin' ev'ry dime to keep you
Talkin' on the line;
That's how it was, and
All those walks together
Out in any kind of weather,
Just because.
There's a brand new way of
Looking at your life, when you
Know that love is standing by your side.

To Chorus:

ARTHUR'S THEME
(Best That You Can Do)

Words and Music by
BURT BACHARACH, CAROLE BAYER SAGER,
CHRISTOPHER CROSS and PETER ALLEN

Moderately
Dm7
G7
F
B♭
E7
A
E/A
A
A/C♯
Dm7
mf
Once in your life, you'll find
Ar - thur, he does what he

G7 C F
her, some-one who turns_ your heart a - round, and
pleas - es. All of his life,_ his mas - ter's toys, and
Bb E7sus4 E7 A
next thing you know, you're clos - in' down the town.
deep in his heart, he's just, he's just a boy.
E/A A A/C# Dm7 G7
Wake up and she's_ still with_ you,
Liv - in' his life_ one day_ at a time, he's
C F Bb
e - ven though you left her way_ a-cross town. You're won - der - in' to your -
show-ing him - self a real - ly good time. He's laugh - in' a - bout the

E7sus4
E7
A
E/A
A
A/C♯
self, hey, what - 've I found?
way they want him to be.
Dmaj7
E/D
4fr.
D
Amaj7
When you get caught be-tween the moon and New York Cit - y,
Bm7
A/B
Bm7
I know it's cra - zy, but it's true.
A
A/C♯
Dmaj7
If you get caught be - tween the

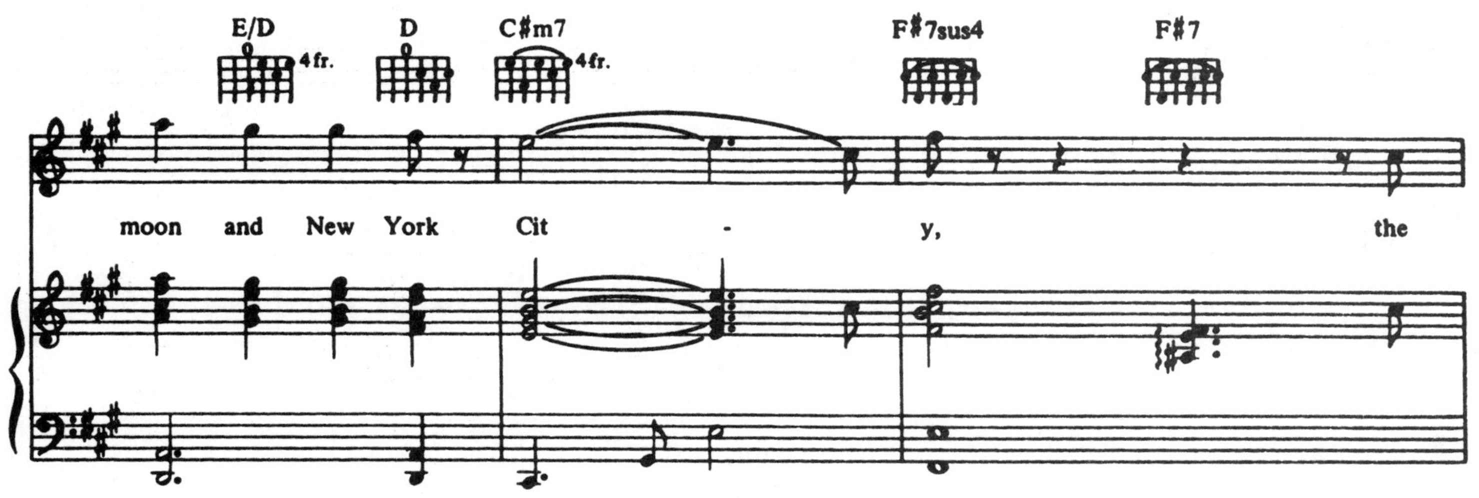

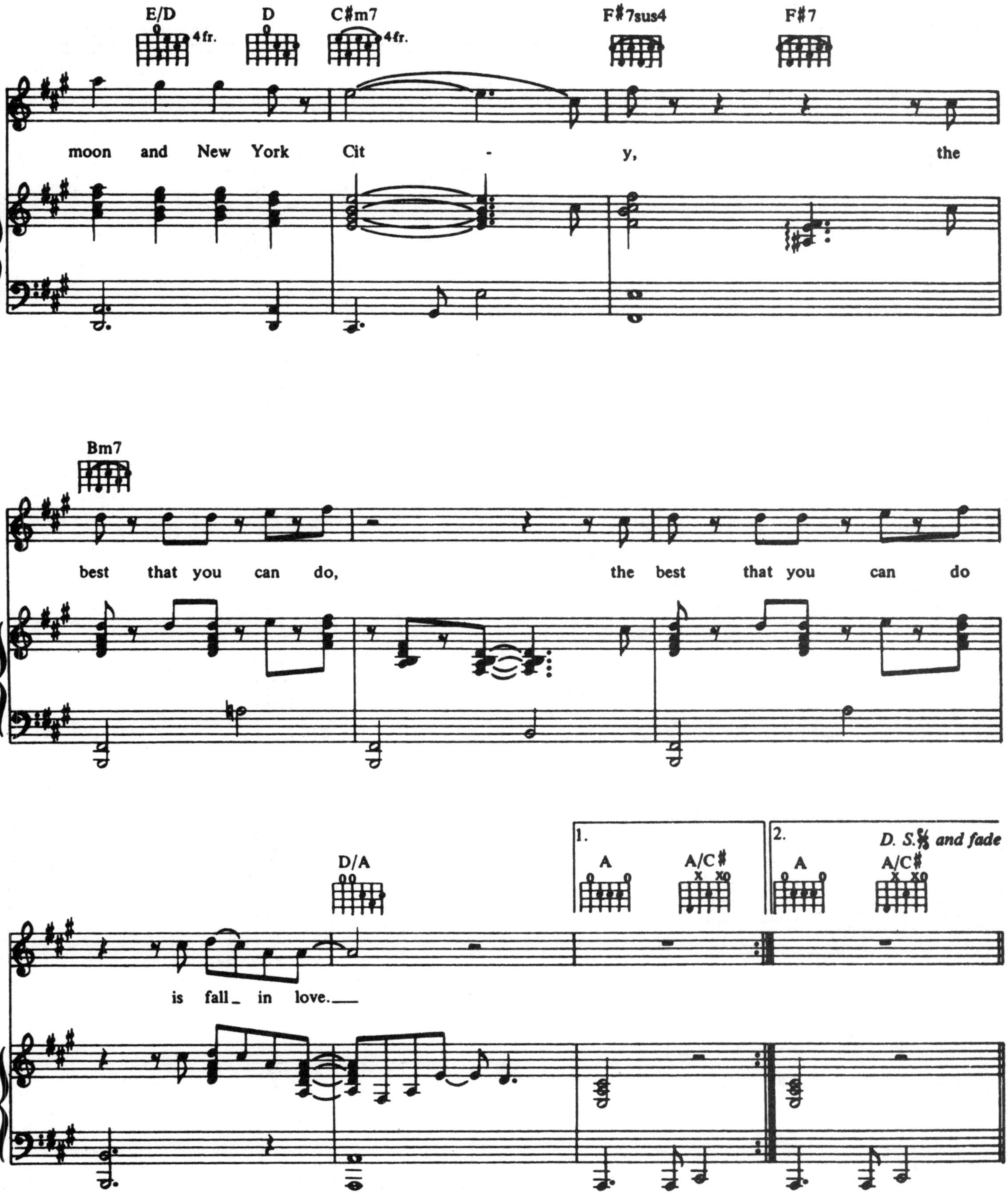

Bm7

best that you can do, the best that you can do

1. 2. *D. S.* 𝄋 *and fade*

D/A A A/C# A A/C#

is fall_ in love.___

BACK IN THE HIGH LIFE AGAIN

Words and Music by
STEVE WINWOOD and
WILL JENNINGS
Moderately, with a beat
D G(addA) D G(addA)
mf
D G(addA) D A D G(addA)
D A D G(addA) D A
It used to seem to me that my life ran on too fast, and I
used to be the best to make life be life to me, and I
D G(addA) D A
had to take it slowly just to make the good parts last. But
hope that you're still out there and you're like you used to be. We'll
Back in the High Life Again - 5 - 1

D
G(addA)
A
when you're born to run it's so hard to just slow down, so
have our-selves a time, and we'll dance till the morn-ing sun, and we'll
don't be sur-prised to see me back in that bright part of town. I'll be
let the good times come in and we won't stop un-til we're done. We'll
A/E
D/F♯
G
back in the high - life a-gain. All the doors I closed
D/A
A7sus4
one time will o-pen up a-gain. I'll We'll be back in the high life a-gain.

D/F♯ G D/A A D G/D D
All the eyes that watched {me/us} once will smile and take {me/us} in. And {I'll/we'll}
G D A D
drink and dance with one hand free, {let the world back in - to me. And / and have the world so eas - i - ly. And}
G D To Coda 1. D/A A
oh, I'll / oh, we'll {be a sight to see back in the high life a - gain.
D G(addA) D G(addA)

D
G(addA)
D
A
You
2.
D/A
A
D
G
high
life
a - gain.
D
A
D
G
1.2.
D
A
3.
D.S. 𝄋 (lyric 2) al Coda
D
A
We'll be
Coda
D/A
A
high
life
a -

D
G(addA)
gain.
High life. Back in the high life.
Oh, we'll be back.
G
Repeat and fade
G/D

CUTS LIKE A KNIFE

Words and Music by
BRYAN ADAMS and
JIM VALLANCE

Moderate Rock ♩ = 100
D
G
C(add2)
f
1.
2.
mf
1. Driv - in' home _ this eve - ning, I could of sworn _ we had it all worked out. _
You

D
G
C(add2)
had this boy be - liev - in' way be -yond the shad - ow of a doubt.
2. Then I
heard it on the street; I heard you might of found some -bod-y new.
3.(See additional lyrics)
C(add 2)
Well,

D
G
C(add2)
who is he, ba - by? Who is he and tell me what he means to
D
you?
4. I
A
Bm
took it all for grant - ed, but how was I to know that
C(add 2)
G
To Coda
you'd be let - ting go? Now it cuts like a

Chorus:
D
G
C(add2)
knife, but it feels so
f
right.___ It cuts like a
knife, but it feels so
1.
C(add 2)
D.S.
right.___ 3. There's

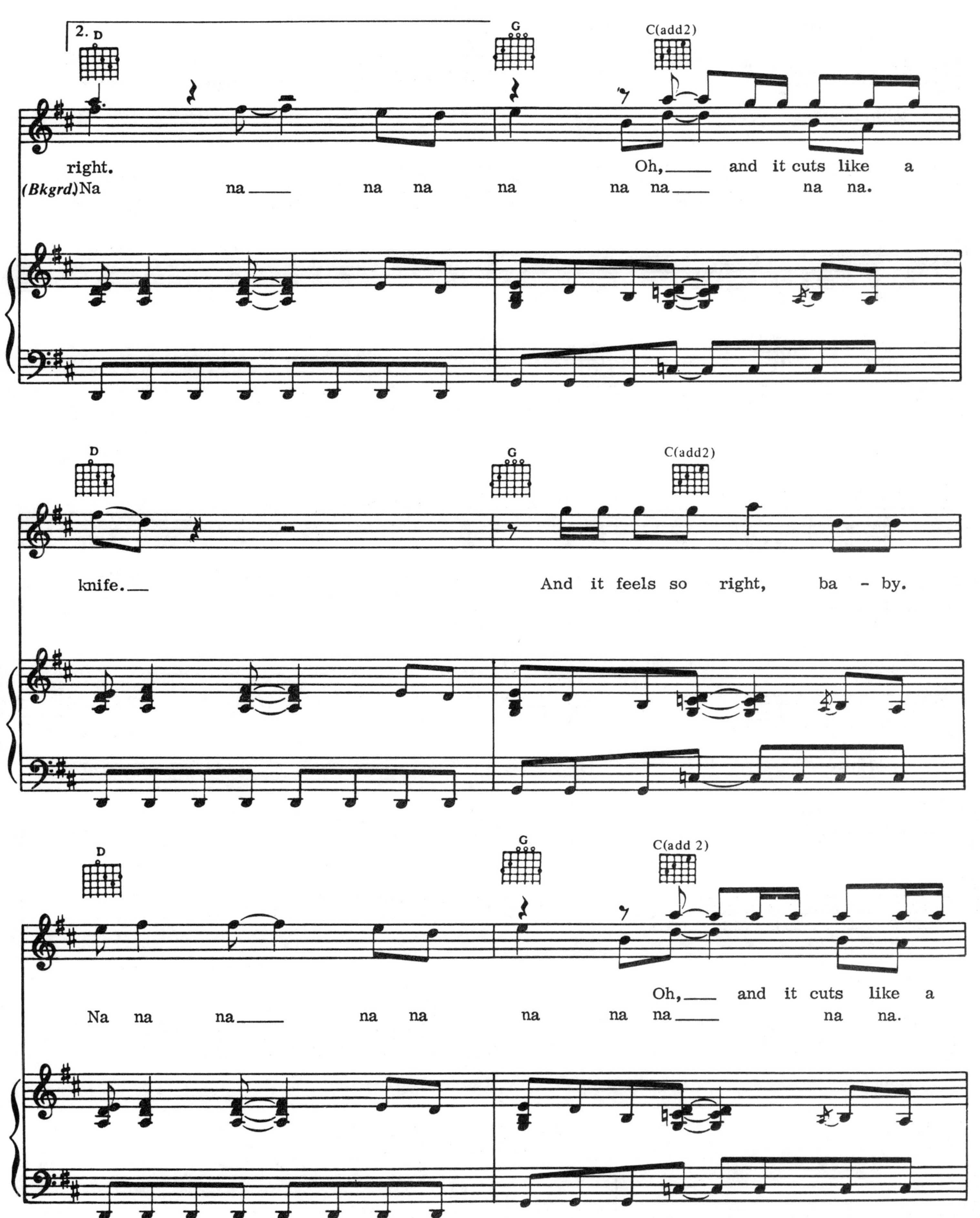
2.
D
G
C(add2)
right.
Oh, and it cuts like a
(Bkgrd.) Na na na na na na na na na.
D
G
C(add2)
knife.
And it feels so right, ba - by.
D
G
C(add 2)
Oh, and it cuts like a
Na na na na na na na na na na.

D
G
C(add 2)
D
knife.
(Instr. Solo ad lib)
G
C(add 2)
D
1. G
C(add2)
2.
D.S.S. al Coda
(End Solo)
4. I
Coda
D
knife,
but it feels so
descresc.
mp
right.
And it cuts like a knife,

Verse 3:
There's times I've been mistaken;
There's times I thought I'd been misunderstood.
So wait a minute darlin'.
Can't you see we did the best we could?
This wouldn't be the first time
Things have gone astray.
Now you've thrown it all away.
(To Chorus:)

DON'T MEAN NOTHING

Lyrics by
RICHARD MARX

Music by
RICHARD MARX and
BRUCE GAITSCH

Medium Rock
C
B♭
mf
R.H.
F
C
B♭
Wel-come to the big_ time. You're bound to be_ a star._ And
F
C
e - ven if you don't go_ all the way,_ I know that you'll_ go far._ This
B♭
F
race is for rats._ It can turn you up-side down. Ain't no one you can count on in this

G
Am
F
G
sleaz - y lit - tle town, oh no.
Lots of prom-is - es in the dark.
Am
Bb
C
But don't you o - pen your heart.
(1.3.) 'Cause it don't mean noth-in',
(2.) But it don't mean noth-in',
the
Bb
F
C
words that they say.
No, it don't mean noth - in', these games that peo-ple play.
Bb
2nd time to Coda I
3rd time to Coda II
No, it don't mean noth-in', no vic - tim, no crime.
No, it don't mean noth-in' till you
*Play cues notes 2nd and 3rd times.
F
C
Bb
sign it on the dot - ted line.

N.C.
C
L.H.
The di-rec-tor smiles as you
Bb
F
walk in the door.__ He
says, "I love your work,__ babe, but you're
C
Bb
just not what we're look-ing for."__
It's nev-er what but
who it is you know.__ So
F
G
eas-y to get stuck in all that
Cal-i-for-nia snow,__ oh.__
Take a
Am
F
G
D.S. al Coda I
Am
Bb
C
good look a-round__ and you'll find__
peo-ple try-in' to
mess with your mind.__

Coda I
F
Am
G/A
3fr.
sign it on the dot - ted line.
Hol - ly - wood can be so lone -
Am
F
ly, make you the win - ner of a los - ing fight.
But the
Am
G/A
3fr.
Am
F
par - ty is nev - er o - ver, 'cause
stars are al - ways shin - ing; does - n't
Am
B♭
C
B♭
mat - ter if it's day or night.
The pro - duc - er says, "Let me
change a line or two,"
and a
F
C
lit - tle bit of some - thing can look
aw - f'lly good to you.

B♭
And you wan-na scream,_ but you got - ta keep it all in - side._ When you're
F
G
try'ng to make_ a liv - ing, there ain't no such thing as pride,_ oh no._
Am
F
G
_ Lots of prom - is - es in_ the dark._ Don't you
Am
B♭
D.S. al Coda II
C
o - pen your heart._
Coda II
F
sign it on the dot - ted line._
C
B♭
F
Repeat and fade
Don't mean noth-in'._ Don't mean noth-in'.

DON'T RUSH ME

Words and Music by
JEFF FRANZEL and
ALEXANDRA FORBES

Cm
Dm
E♭
On - ly time will tell just how well I'll get to know
F
Cm
Dm
you. Don't mean to lead you on, but I want
E♭
D7sus
D7
Chorus:
Gm
to take it slow- ly, slow - ly.
cresc.
So don't rush me.
f
Cm
D7sus
D7
I've made that mis-take be - fore,
ah.
Gm
Cm
Don't rush me. This love could be so much more; it's

Verse 2:
Desire can mean danger.
I wanna lover, not another stranger.
I'm savin' all my passion.
Who's to say if it's love, or just atrraction?
Only time will tell just how well I get to know you.
Don't mean to lead you on, but I want to take it slowly, slowly.
(To Chorus:)

EASY LOVER

Words by
PHIL COLLINS

Music by
PHILIP BAILEY, PHIL COLLINS
and NATHAN EAST

Eb
Fm7
Bbm7
Cm7
3fr.
Fm7
like no oth - er. Be - fore you know it, you'll be on your knees.
Db
4fr.
Eb
Fm7
She's an eas - y lov - er. She'll take your
Bbm7
Cm7
3fr.
Fm7
Db
4fr.
Eb
Fm7
heart, but you won't feel it. She's like no oth - er, and I'm just
Bbm7
Cm7
3fr.
Fm7
Db
4fr.
Cm
3 fr.
Db
4 fr.
try'ng to make you see.
She's the kind of girl you dream of, dream
You're the one that wants to hold her, hold

Eb
Fm
of keep - ing hold of.
her and con - trol her.
Bet - ter for - get it.
Bet - ter for - get it.
Eb
Fm
Cm
3fr.
Db
4 fr.
You'll nev - er get it.
You'll nev - er get it.
She will play
'Cause she'll say
a - round and leave you,
that there's no oth - er
Cm
3fr.
Db
4fr.
leave you and de - ceive you.
till she finds an - oth - er.
Eb
Fm
Eb
Fm
Bet - ter for - get it.
Bet - ter for - get it.
Oh, you'll re -
Oh, you'll re -

Bbm7

gret it.___ No, you'll nev - er change her, so
gret it.___ And don't try to change her. Just

Cm7 3fr. Fm7 Bbm7 Cm7 3fr. Fm7 Bbm7

leave her, leave her. Get out quick 'cause see - ing is be - liev - ing.
leave her, leave her. You're not the on - ly one, and see - ing is be - liev - ing.
It's the

Cm7 3fr. Fm7 Gbmaj13-5

on - ly way___ you'll ev - er know___

1. 2. *D.S.* 𝄋 *and fade*

Db 4fr. Eb Fm7 Eb Fm7

she's___ an eas - y lov-___ an eas - y lov -

DON'T YOU KNOW WHAT THE NIGHT CAN DO?

Words and Music by
STEVE WINWOOD and
WILL JENNINGS

F
C
Hear that_ night mu - sic play - ing?
Time to_ show all your feel - ing,
Don't you_ know what it's
all the_ night is re -
F
C
F
say - ing?
veal - ing.
We should feel_ it to - geth - er,_ for -
Let the rhyth - m_ en - fold you._ Let me
C/G
G
C/G
G
C
ev - er.
hold you.
Feel_ the beat_and just_
Now_ we turn_ in - to_
F
C
G
F
_hold on
_mu - sic.
to the sweet mid - night flow - ing.
Now we nev - er_ will lose it.

C
F
C/G
Feel_ the mu - sic_ in- side_ you._
When_ the rhyth - m_ and night_ ride_
I'll be_ there, too._
no heart_ can hide._
G
Am
C
G
Now's the time when our dreams_ are fi - n'lly com - ing true._
There are times that_ nev - er, ev - er come a - gain._
Am
F
Gsus4
C/G
Am
Feels so good, we're cry - ing._
Mem - 'ries there for mak - ing._
Now's the time_ when it's down_
When the night calls we_ bet -
C
Am
F
C/G
to me_ and you._
ter let_ it in._
Spread those wings,_ we'll be fly - ing.
All this love_ for the tak - ing.

G C/G C/D G7(no3) F/G C/G C/D B°/D C G
Don't you know what the night can do?
F/G C/G B° C G
Don't you know when it's touch - ing you?
1.
F/G C/G B°
Don't you know what the
C G C
night can do?
2.
F/G C/G B° C G
Won't you help me to let it through?
F/A G/B G/C C G G Gsus2 sus4 G
Don't you know what the night can do?

Gsus2 sus4
Am
Em/A
Am
Em/A
Am
F(addG)
G
Am
G/A
3 fr.
Am
G/A
3 fr.
Am
F/C
F
Am/C
G/F
F
Am/G
G
C
F/C
C
F/C
C
Don't you know what the night can do? Know what the night can do? Don't you know
G
Gsus2
G
1.
C/G
G
2.
C/G
G
D.S. 𝄋 and fade (Take 2nd ending)
what the night can do?
Don't you know

ENDLESS SUMMER NIGHTS

Words and Music by
RICHARD MARX

Em
Gm
D
F
All at once I looked and you were gone. And
way your hair would glis - ten in the sun.
C
E♭
Am7
Cm7
now you're look - ing back at me,
Ris - ing in the af - ter - noon,
search - ing for a way that we can be
mak - ing love to you un - der the moon.
G
B♭
F
A♭
like we were be - fore.
Oh.
Do you re -
Em
Gm
D
F
Now I'm back to what I knew be - fore you.
Some -
mem - ber all the nights we spent in si - lence?

Em
Gm
D
F
how the cit - y does - n't look_ the same._
Ev - 'ry sin - gle breath_ you took_ was mine._
I'd
C
E♭
Am7
Cm7
give my life_ for one_ more night_ of
We can have_ it all_ a - gain._
hav-ing you here_ to hold_ me tight._ Oh_ please,_
Say that you'll_ be with_ me when_ the_ sun_
G
B♭
F
A♭
take me there_ a - gain._
brings your heart_ to_ mine._
Oh,_ oh._
Oh,_ oh._
D
F
C
E♭
D
F
G
B♭
C
E♭
And I_
re - mem - ber how_ you loved_

D
C
D
G
C
F
Eb
F
Bb
Eb
me.
Time was all we had un - til the day
Em
D
G
C
Gm
F
Bb
Eb
we said good - bye.
I re - mem - ber ev - 'ry mo -
D
C
D
G
C
F
Eb
F
Bb
Eb
ment of those end - less sum - mer nights.
1. D
C
D
F
Eb
F
I
2. D
G
D/F♯
Em7add4
F
Bb
F/A
Gm7add4

Am7
Cm7
D/F♯
F/A
G
B♭
There's on - ly so much I can say, so please don't run a - way
C
E♭
Am7
Cm7
Dsus4
Fsus4
D
F
from what we have to - geth - er.
Em7add4
Gm7add4
Am7
Cm7
D/F♯
F/A
G
B♭
It's on - ly you and me to - night, so let's stay lost in flight.
C
E♭
Am7
Cm7
C/D
E♭/F
D.S. and fade
Oh, won't you please sur - ren - der. And I

FAITHFULLY

Words and Music by
JONATHAN CAIN

Slow rock ♩ = 66
B
G♯m
mf
B/F♯
E
1. High - way,
B
G♯m
run in - to the mid - night sun.
2. (See additional lyrics)
mp-mf
E
B
Wheels go 'round and 'round; you're on my mind.

3
Rest - less hearts sleep a -
G♯m
E
lone to - night,
send - in' all my love a - long the
B/F♯
F♯
E
G♯m
wire.
They say that the road ain't no place to start a fam-
mf - f
B
Emaj7
G♯m
- 'ly.
Right down the line it's been you and me.

B
E
And lov - in' a mu - sic man _ ain't al - ways what it's
B
F#
D#m
F#
s'pposed to be. _ Oh girl, you stand _ by me. I'm for -
C#m
E
B
ev - er _ yours, _ faith - ful - ly. _ (Instrumental Solo)
mp
G#m
B/F#
1.
E
D.S.
(end solo) 2. Cir - cus

Verse 2:
Circus life
Under the big top world;
We all need the clowns
To make us smile.
Through space and time
Always another show.
Wondering where I am;
Lost without you.

And being apart ain't easy
On this love affair;
Two strangers learn to fall
In love again.
I get the joy
Of rediscovering you.
Oh girl, you stand by me.
I'm forever yours, faithfully.

FOREVER

Words by
KENNY LOGGINS
and EVA EIN LOGGINS

Music by
DAVID FOSTER
and KENNY LOGINS

Bbm/F
F
Cm
3 fr.
Gm
3 fr.
spo - ken. I need - ed to be by your side if on - ly to
fol - low. The love that I lost to the dark I'll al - ways re -
Bb/Ab
Absus2
3 fr.
Bbsus4
Eb
Gm
3 fr.
Cm
3 fr.
Bb
hold you. For - ev - er in my heart,
mem - ber. For - ev - er in my heart,
cresc.
f
Ab
4 fr.
Bbsus4
Bb
Eb
Gm
3 fr.
Cm
3 fr.
Bb
Ab
4 fr.
G/B
for - ev - er we will be, and e - ven when I'm
for - ev - er here you'll be, and know that when I'm
Cm7
3 fr.
Fm7
Fm9
Gm7
3 fr.
Cm7
3 fr.
Fm7(addBb)
Ebsus2/G
Ab6
4 fr.
To Coda
gone, you'll be here in me
gone, you'll be near to me.

Bbm/F F Cm Gm
spo - ken. I need - ed to be by your side if on - ly to
fol - low. The love that I lost to the dark I'll al - ways re -
Bb/Ab Absus2 Bbsus4 Eb Gm Cm Bb
hold you. For - ev - er in my heart,
mem - ber. For - ev - er in my heart,
cresc.
f
Ab Bbsus4 Bb Eb Gm Cm Bb Ab G/B
for - ev - er we will be, and e - ven when I'm
for - ev - er here you'll be, and know that when I'm
Cm7 Fm7 Fm9 Gm7 Cm7 Fm7(addBb) Ebsus2/G Ab6
To Coda
gone, you'll be here in me
gone, you'll be near to me.

B♭sus4
E♭
Gm
Cm
B♭
A♭
E♭sus2/G
Fm7
3 fr.
4 fr.
for - ev - er.
E♭sus2
A♭sus2
Gm7
C7sus4
C7+5
Once I dreamed that you were gone. I cried out try'ng to find
mf
Fm7(addB♭)
B♭7sus4
B♭7
A♭m6/E♭
E♭
you. I begged the dream to fade a - way and please a - wak - en me.
D. S. 𝄋 al Coda ⊕
Coda
G/B
G7/B
B♭sus4
E♭
Gm
Cm
B♭
But
For-ev - er in my life,

Ab
G/B
Cm7
F9
al - ways thought I'd be,
I'd be yours
dim.
Eb/Bb
Bb
Ab/Bb
mf
G7/B
Cm
Bb/C
Gm7
Fm7
Ebmaj7/G
Absus2
Eb/G
for - ev - er.
f
ff

Eb
Gm
3 fr.
Cm
3 fr.
Bb
Ab
4 fr.
Bbsus4
Bb
Eb
Gm
3 fr.
Cm
3 fr.
Bb
Ab
4 fr.
Bbsus4
Bb
Eb
Gm
3 fr.
Cm
3 fr.
Bb
Ab
4 fr.
Bbsus4
Bb
Eb
Bb/D
Cm
3 fr.
Bbsus4
Absus2
3 fr.
Gm
3 fr.
Fm7
Ebmaj7/G
Ab
4 fr.
Bb(addEb)
Eb

FOREVER I DO
(The Wedding Song)

Words and Music by
DEXTER WANSEL and CYNTHIA BIGGS

*The 1st verse may be sung freely, out of tempo.

Bridge:

D F♯m7 Gmaj7 Asus

mf

Do I take you this mo - ment,

D C/D D/A D(9) E/G♯ F♯7 - 9

and — for my whole life through? Do I prom - ise to

Bm7 D7 Gmaj7 Gmaj7/A D

love you? — For - ev - er I do, for - ev - er I do.

A/C♯ *Chorus:* F♯m7 Bm7 F/G Em7/A

cresc. *f*

For - ev - er I do; I'll al - ways love you. For -

F♯m7 Bm7 F/G Em7/A

ev er I do; I prom - ise to be true. For -

Verse 2:
This band of gold to have and to hold
I give to you as my token of my devotion.
I'll take your hand, and we will stand
Here in the eyes of the beholders together.

Bridge 2:
Do I promise to love you?
And for my whole life through,
Do I take you from this moment?
Forever I do, for ever I do.

(To Chorus:)

HELLO

Words and Music by
LIONEL RICHIE

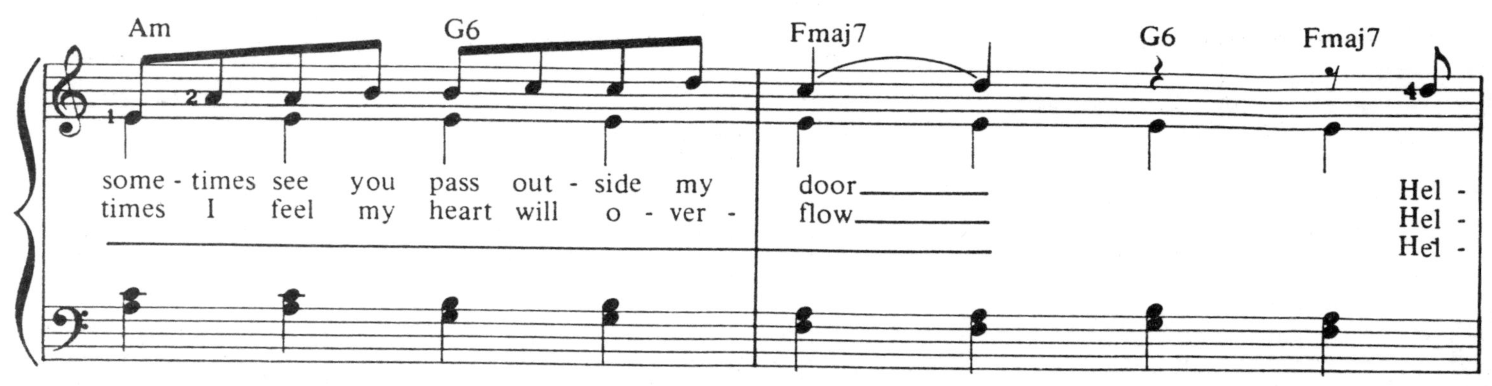
Am
G6
Fmaj7
G6
Fmaj7
some - times see you pass out - side my door
times I feel my heart will o - ver - flow
Hel -
Hel -
Hel -

Am
G6
Fmaj7
A
lo is it me you're look - ing for? I can
lo I've just got to let you know 'cause I
lo is it me you're look - ing for? 'cause I

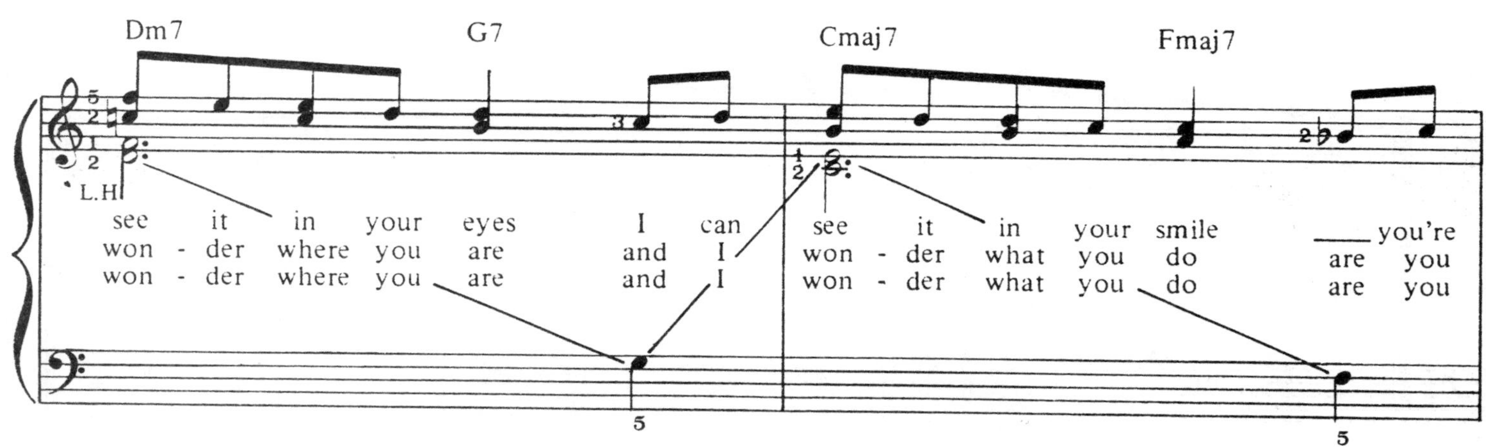
Dm7
G7
Cmaj7
Fmaj7
L.H.
see it in your eyes I can see it in your smile you're
won - der where you are and I won - der what you do are you
won - der where you are and I won - der what you do are you

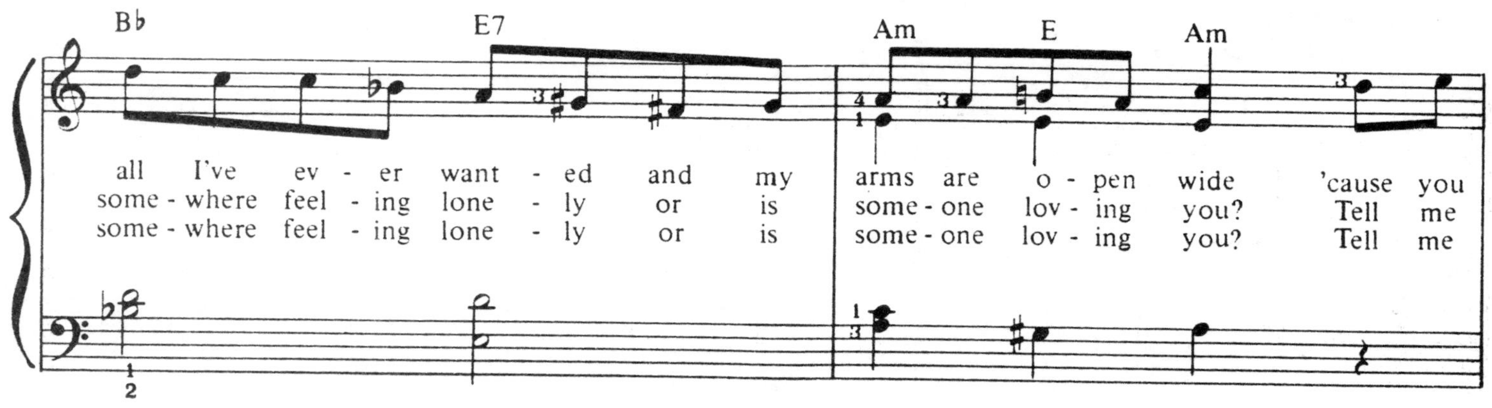
B♭
E7
Am
E
Am
all I've ev - er want - ed and my arms are o - pen wide 'cause you
some - where feel - ing lone - ly or is some - one lov - ing you? Tell me
some - where feel - ing lone - ly or is some - one lov - ing you? Tell me

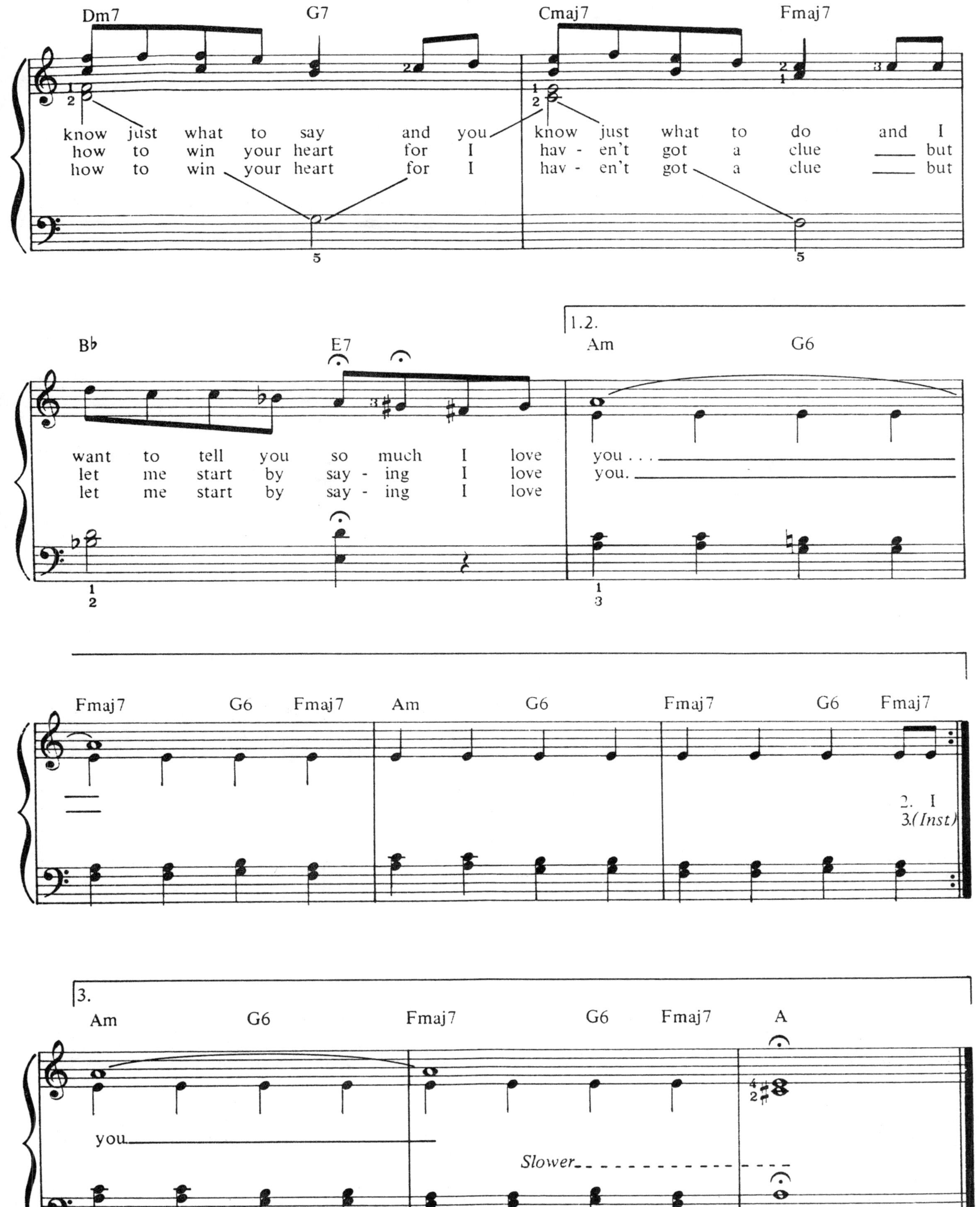
Dm7
G7
Cmaj7
Fmaj7
know just what to say and you know just what to do and I
how to win your heart for I hav - en't got a clue but
how to win your heart for I hav - en't got a clue but
B♭
E7
1.2.
Am
G6
want to tell you so much I love you . . .
let me start by say - ing I love you.
let me start by say - ing I love
Fmaj7
G6
Fmaj7
Am
G6
Fmaj7
G6
Fmaj7
2. I
3.(Inst)
3.
Am
G6
Fmaj7
G6
Fmaj7
A
you
Slower

FROM A DISTANCE

Lyrics and Music by
JULIE GOLD

G D/G G Cmaj7 D Em
flight. From a dis-tance there is har - mo-ny, and it
cresc. mf
C G/B G/D D C G/B C G/B
To Coda
ech-oes through the land. It's the voice of hope, it's the voice of peace. It's the
dim. mp
C D
1.
G D/G C/G G
voice of ev - ery man.
C G/B D
D.S.
2.
G D/G G G/B
Bridge:
G/C C6 D
2. From a man. God is watch-ing us. God is
cresc. mf
D7/G G D/F# Em Em7 Am7 C/D D G
watch-ing us. God is watch-ing us from a dis - tance.
dim. mp

G G/B C D
Em7 G/B C G/B Am Em/G D/F♯ D
D.S. 𝄋 al Coda
G D/F♯ C/E G/D C Am Em D Em D/F♯ N.C.
cresc.
mf
3. From a
mp
Coda
C D7 D/E Em D/E Em Bm/D
heart of ev - ery man. It's the
cresc.
mf
C G/B C G/B C D7
hope of hopes, it's the love of loves. This is the song of ev - ery

Verse 2:
From a distance, we all have enough,
And no one is in need.
There are no guns, no bombs, no diseases,
No hungry mouths to feed.
From a distance, we are instruments
Marching in a common band;
Playing songs of hope, playing songs of peace,
They're the songs of every man.
(To Bridge:)

Verse 3:
From a distance, you look like my friend
Even though we are at war.
From a distance I just cannot comprehend
What all this fighting is for.
From a distance there is harmony
And it echos through the land.
It's the hope of hopes, it's the love of loves.
It's the heart of every man.

HEAVEN

Words and Music by
BRYAN ADAMS and
JIM VALLANCE

Slow Rock ♩ = 66
mp
with pedal
C
Am7
G
1. Oh, think-in' a-bout all our young-er years; there was
2. Oh, once in your life you will find some-one who will
mp
Dm
Am
B♭add 2
Gsus
G
on-ly you and me; we were young and wild and free.
turn your world a-round; bring you up when you're feel-ing down.

C
Am7
G
Now noth - ing can take___ you a - way from me;___ we've been
Yeah, noth - ing could change_ what you mean to me.___ Oh, there's
Dm
Am
B♭add 2
F/A
down that road be - fore,_ but that's o - ver now;_ you keep me
lots that I could say;_ just hold me now,_ 'cause our
Gsus
G
F
G
Am
com-in' back for more._ Ba-by, you're all___ that I want when you're
love will light the way;_ And ba-by,
f
C
F
G
Am
ly - in' here_ in my arms. I'm find-ing it hard___ to be - lieve we're in
simile

G
F
G
Am
heav - en.
And love is all__ that I need, and I
C
F
G
Am
found it there__ in your heart.
It is - n't too hard__ to see__ we're in
1.
Gno 3rd
C
Am
C/G
F add 2
D.S.
heav-en.
mp
2. G
To next strain
3. G
Repeat ad. lib. and fade
heav-en.
heav - en, heav- en.____

Dm
C/E
F
G
I've been wait-ing for so long for some-thing to ar-rive;
Am
G/B
C
Dm
C/E
for love to come a-long.
Now our dreams are com-in' true,
F
C
Gsus
G
through the good times and the bad.
Yeah, I'll be stand-in' there by you.
F
G
Am
C
F
G
Am
G
D.S.S.
And
Instrumental solo
-------end solo

HOLD ON TO THE NIGHTS

Words and Music by
RICHARD MARX

Am
Cm
Fsus2/A
A♭sus2/C
Gsus4
B♭sus4
G
B♭
this ev - er-chang - ing world push - es me through an - oth - er door.
Prom - is - es in vain, love that is real, but in dis - guise.
Gsus2
B♭sus2
G
B♭
Dm7add4
Fm7add4
Fsus2
A♭sus2
I saw you smile and my
What hap - pens now? Do we
Gsus4
B♭sus4
G
B♭
Gsus4
B♭sus4
G
B♭
Dm7add4
Fm7add4
mind could not e - rase the beau - ty of your face. Just for a while
break an - oth - er rule, let our lov - ers play the fool? I don't know how
Play 1st time only
Fsus2
A♭sus2
Gsus2/B
B♭sus2/D
Fsus2/A
A♭sus2/C
Gsus4
B♭sus4
G
B♭
won't you let me shel - ter you?
to

*Vocalists: Hold C for 4 beats.

2.
C/E
E♭/G
F
A♭
Gsus4
B♭sus4
G
B♭
If on - ly I could give you more.
Well, I
Bm
Dm
A
C
think that I've been true to ev - 'ry - bod - y else but me.
And the
Dm7
Fm7
G
B♭
way I feel a - bout you makes my heart long to be free.
Ev - 'ry
Bm
Dm
A
C
time I look in - to your eyes, I'm help - less - ly a - ware that the

Dm7
Fm7
F6
A♭6
E/G♯
G/B
some - one I've — been search - ing for — is right there. —
D/F♯
F/A
Bm
Dm
A/B
C/D
Bm
Dm
A
C
G
B♭
A
C
D/F♯
F/A
G
B♭
Asus4
Csus4
A
C
cresc.
f
Hold on — to the nights. —
D/F♯
F/A
G
B♭
Asus4
Csus4
A
C
Hold on — to the mem - o - ries. —

Bm7
Dm7
G
B♭
Asus4
Csus4
A
C
I wish that I could give you more.
D/F♯
F/A
Oh.
Hold on to the nights.
8va

HOW WILL I KNOW

Words and Music by
GEORGE MERRILL, SHANNON RUBICAM,
and NARADA MICHAEL WALDEN

1.
2.3.
D
G
G(9)/B
Am11
C
Cmaj7
Bm7
G/B
G/D
Em
Chorus:
2. Oh, I lose
How will I know?
(Girl, trust your feel - ings.) How will I know?
How will I know? (Love can be de - ceiv - in'.) How will I know?
How will I know if he real - ly loves me?
I say a prayer with ev - ery heart - beat.
I fall in love when - ev -

Em7
G
Bm7
Cmaj7
D
G/D
-er we meet.
I'm ask-in' you, 'cause you know a-bout these things.
Em
How will I know if he's think-in' of me?
I try to phone, but I'm
too shy. (Can't speak.)
Fall-ing in love is so bit-ter-sweet.
1.
D.S.
2.
To next strain
G/B
C/D
This love is strong. Why do I feel weak? 3. Oh, wake I feel weak? If he loves
3.4. etc.
Repeat ad lib. and fade
I feel weak? me; if he loves

Verse 3:
Oh, wake me, I'm shakin'; wish I had you near me now.
Said there's no mistakin'; what I feel is really love.
How will I know? (Girl, trust your feelings.)
How will I know?
How will I know? (Love can be deceiving.)
How will I know?

**Repeat Chorus in key of "E"*

I KNEW YOU WERE WAITING
(FOR ME)

Words and Music by
DENNIS MORGAN and
SIMON CLIMIE

F#m7
C#m7
Some-how I made it through the heart-ache;
F#m7
C#m7
F#m7
I es-caped.
I found my way out of the
C#m7
A
E
dark-ness; kept my faith, kept my faith. When the riv-er was deep,
cresc.
Chorus:
A/E
E
A/E
I did-n't fal-ter; when the moun-tain was high, I still be-lieved.
f

E
A/E
When the val - ley was low, it did-n't stop me, no, no. I
F#m7
C#m7
1.
A
knew you were wait - ing, I knew you were wait - ing for me.
D.S.
2. With an end - less de - sire,
mf
2.
To next strain
3.4. etc.
Repeat ad lib. and fade
A/C#
knew you were wait - ing for me.
So we were drawn

Verse 2:
With an endless desire, I kept on searchin', sure in time our eyes would meet.
Now like bridges on fire the hurt is over, one touch and you set me free.
I don't regret a single moment, oh, oh, lookin' back,
When I think of all those disappointments, I just laugh.
(To Chorus:)

I WILL ALWAYS LOVE YOU

Words and Music by
DOLLY PARTON

Verse 2:
Bitter sweet memories, that's all I have and all I'm taking with me.
Good-bye, oh please don't cry, 'cause we both know that I'm not what you need, but . . .
(To Chorus:)

Verse 3: ***(Recite)***
And I hope life will treat you kind, and I hope that you have all that you ever dreamed of.
Oh, I do wish you joy, and I wish you happiness, but above all this, I wish you love;
I love you, I will always love you. (To Chorus:)

IF EVER YOU'RE IN MY ARMS AGAIN

Words and Music by
MICHAEL MASSER, TOM SNOW
and CYNTHIA WEIL

D(add2)
And I still can re - mem - ber how you
There's some - thing be - tween us that
G6/D
touched me so ten - der. It told me you care.
won't ev - er leave us. There's no let - ting go.
C
Fmaj7
F6
We had a once in a life - time, but I
We had a once in a life - time, but I
mf
Dm
Am
C
G
just could - n't see un - til it was gone.
just did - n't know it till my life fell a - part.

C
Fmaj7
F6
A sec - ond once in a life - time; may be
A sec - ond once in a life - time is - n't
Dm
Am
C
G
A
too much to ask. But I swear from now on
too much to ask. 'Cause I swear from now on
Chorus: D
D/F♯
Gmaj7
A
F♯m7
Bm7
if ev - er you're in my arms a - gain, this time I'll love
f
Em7
G
A
D
D/F♯
Gmaj7
A
you much bet - ter. If ev - er you're in my arms a - gain,

F♯m7 Bm7 Em7

this time ___ I'll hold ___ you for - ev - er.

1. G/A A Dsus(add 2) 2fr D Dsus(add 2) 2fr D

This time will nev - er end. Ooo. ___

mf

E7sus Em7 Esus(add 2) Em7/A D.S. 𝄋

2. G/A A

2. Now This time we'll nev - er end, ___

Bm7 Bm6

___ nev - - er end. ___

mf

Bm7
Bm6
The
G
D/F#
best of ro - manc - in de - serves sec - ond chanc - es. I'll
Em7
G/A
B
get to you some - how. 'Cause I prom - ise now.
E
E/G#
Amaj7
B
(end.) If ev - er you're in my arms a - gain

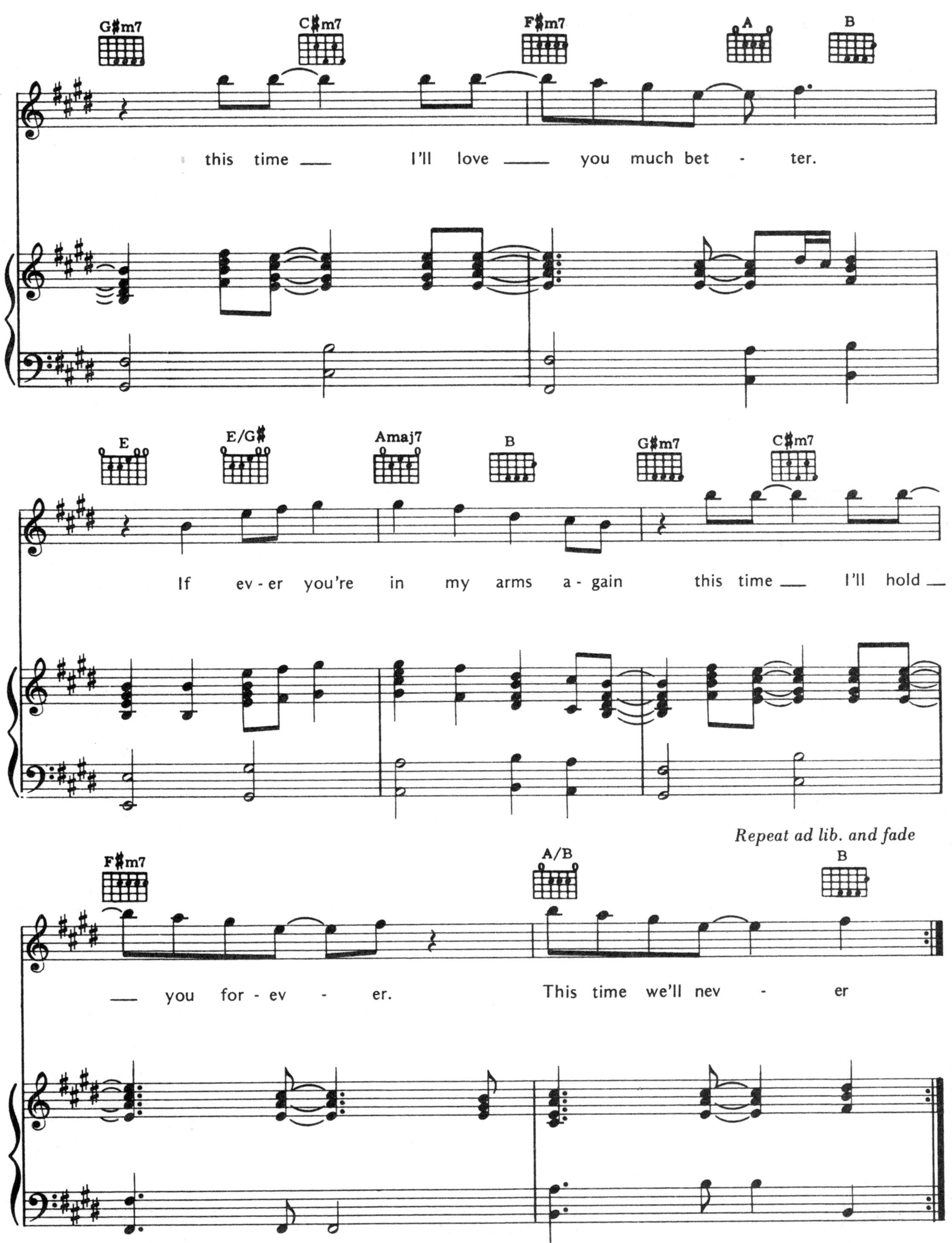
G♯m7
C♯m7
F♯m7
A
B
this time ___ I'll love ___ you much bet - ter.
E
E/G♯
Amaj7
B
G♯m7
C♯m7
If ev - er you're in my arms a - gain this time ___ I'll hold ___
Repeat ad lib. and fade
F♯m7
A/B
B
___ you for - ev - er. This time we'll nev - er

IN THE AIR TONIGHT

Words and Music by
PHIL COLLINS

C/D
Bb/D
C/D
ing in the air to-night, oh Lord, oh Lord?
Dm
Well, if
Dm
Am/D
you told me you were drown-ing, I would not lend a hand.
Bb/D
I've seen your face be-fore, my friend, but I don't

F/D
Dm
know if you know who I am.
Well, I was there and I saw
Am/D
what you did.
I saw it with my own two eyes.
So you can
B♭/D
wipe off that grin.
I know where you've been.
It's
F/D
Dm
all been a pack of lies.
And I can feel it com-

C/D
Bb/D
C/D
ing in the air to-night, oh Lord.
Dm
C/D
Well, I've been wait - ing for this moment for all my life,
Bb/D
C/D
Dm
oh Lord. I can feel it com-
C/D
Bb/D
C/D
ing in the air to-night, oh Lord.

Dm
C/D
B♭/D
Well, I've been wait-ing for this mo-ment for all my life, oh Lord,
C/D
Dm
oh Lord.
Dm
Well, I re-mem-ber, I re-
Am/D
mem-ber, don't wor-ry. How could I ev-er for-get? It's the

Bb/D
F/D
first time, — the last time — we ev-er met.
Dm
But I — know the rea-son — why — you keep the si-lence up.
Am/D
Bb/D
No, you don't fool me. The hurt does-n't show, but the
F/D
D.S. and fade
pain — still grows. — It's no stran-ger to you — or me.

I WANNA DANCE WITH SOMEBODY (WHO LOVES ME)

Words and Music by
GEORGE MERRILL and
SHANNON RUBICAM

C
F/A
C/Bb
F/Bb Bb
Gm7
F/A
C/D
till now; it's the light of day that shows me how. But when the night falls
Bb F/A Bb C
Chorus:
F
3
lone - li - ness calls.
f
Oh, I wan-na dance with some-bod - y.
I wan-na feel the heat with some-bod - y.
Dm7
Yeah, I wan-na dance
with some-bod - y,
Bbmaj7
with some - bod - y who loves me.
C7sus
F
Oh, I wan-na dance with some-bod - y.
I wan-na feel the heat

Dm7

with some-bod - y. Yeah, I wan-na dance with some-bod - y,

1.

B♭maj7 Gm7 Am B♭6 C7sus F

with some - bod - y who loves me.

D.S. 𝄋 | 2. To next strain | 3.4. etc. Repeat ad lib. and fade

Gm7 Am B♭6 C7sus Gm7 Am B♭6 C7sus

bod - y who loves me. Some- bod - y who loves me.

Bridge:

Dm9 | 1. C

- bod-y, ooo, some - bod-y, ooo; some-bod - y who loves

2. D.S.S. 𝄋𝄋

Gm Am C B♭ Am7

me. to hold me in his arms.

Verse 2:
I've been in love and lost my senses
Spinning through the town.
Sooner or later the fever ends,
And I wind up feeling down.
I need a man who'll take a chance
On a love that burns hot enough to last.
So when the night falls,
My lonely heart calls.
(To Chorus:)

Verse 3:
I need a man who'll take a chance
On a love that burns hot enought to last.
So when the night falls,
My lonely heart calls.
(To Chorus:)

KEY LARGO

Words and Music by
BERTIE HIGGINS and
SONNY LIMBO

Moderately ♩= 84

8va

mf

8va

Am
C
C/D

p

1. Wrapped a - round_each oth - er, Try-in' so hard to__ stay__
2. *(See additional lyrics)*

Gmaj9
Am
warm; That first cold win - ter to - geth - er,
C
C/D
Gmaj9
Ly - in' in each oth - er's arms; Watch - ing those old
Em
mov - ies, Fall - ing in love so des - per -
Cmaj7
ate - ly; Hon - ey, I was your

Am7
C/D
he - ro, And you were my lead - ing la - dy.
Chorus:
G
Bm
We had it all,
C
C/D
G
Bm
Just like Bo - gie and Ba - call;
(sim.)
C
C/D
G
Em
Star - ring in our own late, late show,

C
C/D
G
Bm
Sail-ing a-way to Key Lar - go.
C
C/D
G
Bm
Here's look-ing at you kid,
C
C/D
G
Bm
Miss-ing all the things we did;
C
C/D
G
Em
We can find it once a-gain I know,

Verse 2:
Honey, can't you remember
Playin' all the parts;
That sweet scene of surrender,
When you gave me your heart?
Please say you will
Play it again;
'Cause I love you still.
Baby, this can't be the end.

SHOW ME THE WAY

Lyrics and Music by
DENNIS DE YOUNG

G♭ A♭m7 D♭/F E♭m C♭ D♭sus D♭
feel this emp - ty place in - side; so a - fraid that I've lost my faith. Show me the
mf
Chorus:
G♭ D♭ C♭ G♭ D♭ C♭
way, show me the way.
Take me to - / Bring me to -
f
G♭ D♭/F E♭m7 G♭/D♭ A♭m7 D♭sus D♭
To Coda
night to the riv - er and wash my il - lu - sions a - way.
night to the moun-tain and take my con - fu - sion a - way.
Please show me the
G♭ C♭/G♭ D♭/G♭ C♭/G♭
way.
1. D.S.
G♭ C♭/G♭ D♭/G♭ C♭/G♭
2. And
2.
G♭ C♭/G♭ D♭/G♭ C♭
Bridge:
B♭ E♭m
and if I see a light, should I be - lieve? Tell me, how will I

A♭7 A♭m7
D♭sus D♭ D♭sus D♭
A B/A Amaj7 B/A
know?
D.S.S. al Coda
A B/A
A B/A Amaj7 B/A
D♭ C♭/D♭ D♭ C♭/D♭
Show me the
Coda
G♭ D♭ C♭
G♭ D♭ C♭
way, show me the way. Take me to -
G♭ D♭/F E♭m7 G♭/D♭
A♭m7 D♭sus D♭
night to the riv - er and wash my il - lu - sions a - way. Show me the
G♭ D♭ C♭
G♭ D♭ C♭
way, show me the way. Give me the

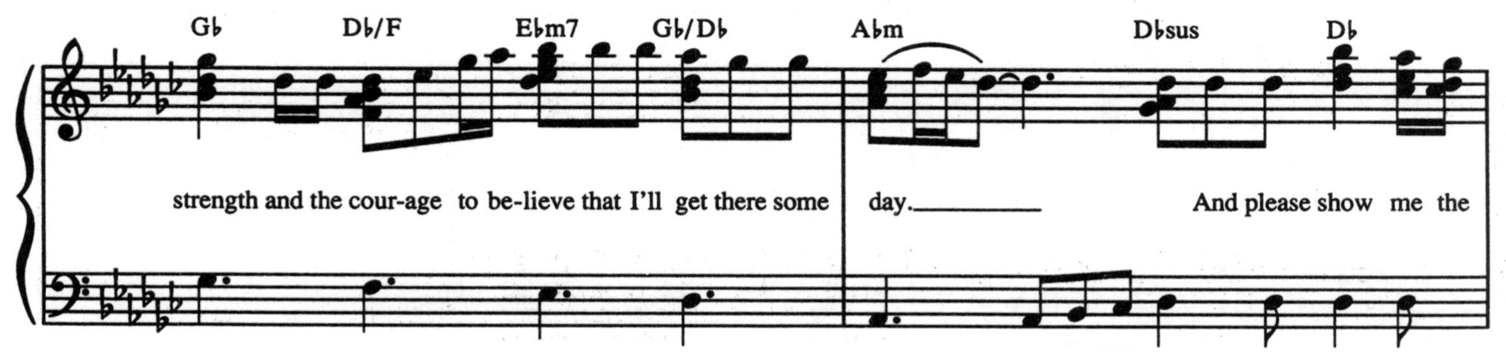
Gb Db/F Ebm7 Gb/Db Abm Dbsus Db
strength and the cour-age to be-lieve that I'll get there some day.
And please show me the

Gb Cb/Gb Db/Gb Cb/Gb Gb Cb/Gb Db/Gb Cb/Gb Gb Cb/Gb Gb Db/Gb

way.

mf

mp *Slower*

G Abm7 Db/F Gb Ebm Cbmaj7 Dbsus Db

p

Ev - 'ry night I say a pray'r in the hopes that there's a heav-en.

Verse 2:
And as I slowly drift to sleep
For a moment dreams are sacred.
I close my eyes and know there's peace
In a world so filled with hatred.
Then I wake up each morning and turn on the news
To find we've so far to go.
And I keep on hoping for a sign
So afraid I just won't know.
(To Chorus:)

THE LADY IN RED

Words and Music by
CHRIS DeBURGH

Gm
Bb7/F
Eb
Cm7
mance, giv-en half ___ a chance. I have nev-er seen that dress you're wear-ing, or the
F7
Gm
high-lights in ___ your hair ___ that catch ___ your eyes. ___ I have ___ been blind ___
F
F7/Eb
Chorus:
Bb
Bb/D
Ebadd2
F
___ The la - dy in red ___ is danc - ing ___ with
mf
Gm
F/A
Gm
me, cheek ___ to cheek. ___ There's no - bod - y here, ___

Cm7
Fadd9
B♭
it's just you and me.
It's where I wan-na be.
B♭7
E♭
D7/F♯
D7
But I hard-ly know
this beau-ty by my side.
cresc.
f
Gm
Gm/F
C7/E
Cm7
I'll nev-er for-get
dim.
mf
Fadd9
F
B♭
D.S.
the way you look to-night.
dim.
p

Verse 2:
I've never seen you looking so gorgeous as you did tonight;
I've never seen you shine so bright.
You were amazing.
I've never seen so many people want to be there by your side,
And when you turned to me and smiled,
It took my breath away.
I have never had such a feeling,
Such a feeling of complete and utter love
As I do tonight.

(To Chorus:)

LIKE A ROCK

Words and Music by
BOB SEGER

Gb(add2)
Db
4fr.
The height of sum-mer, I'd nev-er felt that strong, like a
Ab
Db/Ab
Ab
Ab
rock.
I was eigh-teen,
Db
did-n't have a care.
Work-in' for pea-nuts,
Gb(add2)
not a dime to spare,
but I was lean and

Db
4fr.
Ab
4fr.
Db/Ab
4 fr.
Ab
4fr.
Db/Ab
4fr.
sol - id ev - 'ry - where, like a rock.
Ab
4fr.
3. My hands were stead - y, My eyes were clear and bright.
Db
4fr.
My walk had pur - pose, my steps were quick and light,
Gb(add2)
Db
4fr.
To Coda
and I held firm to what I felt was right, like a

Ab
4fr.
Db/Ab
4 fr.
Ab
4fr.
Ab
4fr.
mf
rock. Like a rock, I was
Db
4fr.
strong as I ___ could be; ___ like a rock, noth-in'
Gb(add2)
ev - er got ___ to me; ___ like a rock, I was
Db
4fr.
Ab
4fr.
Db/Ab
4 fr.
Ab
4fr.
some-thin' to see, ___ like a rock. And I

Fm
stood ar - row straight un - en - cum-bered by the weight of all these
f
A♭
4fr.
hus - tlers and their schemes;
I stood proud,
D♭
4fr.
I stood tall,
high a - bove it all.
I
3
B♭m7
E♭
(let ring)
still be - lieved in my dreams.

Solo

Ab 4fr. — Db 4fr. — Gb/Db

ff

Db 4fr. — Gb(add2) — Db 4fr. — Ab 4fr. — Bbm/Ab

1. Ab 4fr. — 2. Ab 4fr. *(Let ring)* — Ab 4fr. — Ab/Db 4fr.

mp

D. S. 𝄋 *al Coda* 𝄌

Ab 4fr. — Ab/Db 4fr. — Ab 4fr. — Ab/Db 4fr. — Ab 4fr. — Ab/Db 4fr.

Repeat and fade

Coda 𝄌

Ab 4fr. — Ab 4fr.

call, I re - call like a rock,
rock, the

3

f

4. Twenty years now;
Where'd they go?
Twenty years;
I don't know.
I sit and I wonder sometimes
Where they've gone.

5. And sometimes late at night,
When I'm bathed in the firelight,
The moon comes callin' a ghostly
white,
And I recall.

MAN IN THE MIRROR

Words and Music by
SIEDAH GARRETT and GLEN BALLARD

Medium

No Chord
p
Pedal

I'm gon - na make a change,
for once in my life.

It's gon-na feel real good, gon-na make a diff-erence, gon-na make it right.

As I turn up the col - lar on
my fav-orite win - ter coat,
this wind is blow-in' my mind.
I see the kids
in the street
with not e - nough to eat.
Who am I
to be blind?
Pre-tend-ing not to
see their needs.
Am7(addD)
G/B
A sum-mer's dis - re - gard,
a bro - ken bot - tle top,

C(addD)
G/B
Am7(addD)
and a one ___ man's soul. ___ They fol - low each oth - er on the wind,
G/B
C(addD)
C/D
ya' know, 'cause they got ___ no - where to go, that's why I want you to know.
G
G(addA)/B
C
C/D
G
G(addA)/B
I'm start - ing with the man ___ in the mir-ror, I'm ask - ing him to
mf
C
C/D
G
G(addA)/B
C
A/C♯
change his ways. And no ___ mes-sage could have been an - y clear-er: {If you (If you

D7+9
4fr.
C/D
wan-na make the world a bet - ter place, take a look at your-self, and then make a change.
wan-na make the world a bet - ter place,) (take a look at your-self, and then make a change.)
G
D/F#
Em7
D
C(addD)
(Na na na, na na na, na na, na nah.)
D
Em7
D/F#
G
D/F#
Em7
D
I've been a vic - tim of a self - ish kind of love,
C(addD)
G
D/F#
It's time that I re - al - ize, that there are some with no home, not a

Em7
D
C(addD)
nick-el to loan. Could it be real-ly me, pre-tend-ing that they're not a - lone?
Am7(addD)
G/B
C(addD)
A wil-low deep-ly scarred, some-bod-y's brok-en heart, and a washed out dream,
G(addA)/B
Am7(addD)
G/B
They fol-low the pat-tern of the wind, ya' see, 'cause they got
(Washed out dream.)
C(addD)
C/D
no place to be, that's why I'm start - ing with me.
(Start - ing with me!)

Michael:
G
G(addA)/B
C
C/D
G
G(addA)/B
I'm starting with the man in the mirror, I'm asking him to
Chorus:
(Ooh!)
C
C/D
G
G(addA)/B
change his ways.
And no mes - sage could have / could-'ve
(Change his ways
(Ooh!) ooh!)
C
A/C#
D7+9
4fr.
been an - y clear-er: If you wan-na make the world a bet - ter place, take a
(If you wan-na make the world a bet - ter place,) (take a
(#)

1.
G/D
look at your - self and then make a change.
look at your - self and then make a change)
2.
Ab
4fr.
Ab(addBb)/C
look at your-self and then make that I'm start - ing with the
look at your-self and then make that... change!
Db
4fr.
Db/Eb
Ab
4fr.
Ab(addBb)/C
man in the mir-ror, I'm ask - ing him to
(Man in the mir-ror, oh, yeah!)

Db
Db/Eb
Ab
Ab(addBb)/C
4fr.
change ___ his ways. ___
No ___ mes - sage could have
(Bet- ter change!)
(Oh ___
Db
Bb/D
Eb7 + 9
5fr.
been an - y clear-er.
___)
(If you wan- na make the world a bet - ter place,) (take a
look at your - self and then make the change. _) (You got - ta

Eb7(+9)(+5)
5fr.
You can't close your, your
get it right, while you got the time___) ('Cause when you close your heart___) (then you close your
Ab
4fr.
Ab(addBb)/C
Db
4fr.
Db/Eb
With that man___ in the mir-ror,
mind! That man, that man, that man,___ that
mind!) (Man___ in the mir-ror, oh
I'm ask-ing him to change___ his ways.___
man, that man, that man, that man. You
yeah!) (Bet-ter

Ab
Ab(addBb)/C
Db
Bb/D
4fr.
No, mes - sage could have been an - y clear-er.
know, that man.
If you
change!)
(If you
Eb7+9
5fr.
wan - na make the world a bet - ter place, take a
wan - na make the world a bet - ter place,) (take a
look at your - self and then make a
look at your - self and then make a

A♭
4fr.
Hoo!
E♭/G
Hoo!
Fm7
Hoo!
E♭
Hoo!
change.
Na na na, na na na, na
change.)
D♭(addE♭)
Hoo!
na, na nah.
Gon-na feel real good now!
A♭
4fr.
E♭/G
Yeah yeah!
Fm7
Yeah
(Oh yeah!)
yeah!
E♭
Yeah yeah!
D♭(addE♭)
Oh no, no no.
Na na na, na na na, na na, na nah.
(Ooooh.)

D♭(addE♭)
I'm gon - na make a change,
It's gon-na feel real good!
Come on!
(Change.
)
Just lift your - self,
you know.
You've got to stop it.
Your -
Play 4 times (See addtitional lyrics)
self!
I've got to make that
(Yeah!
Make that
change!)

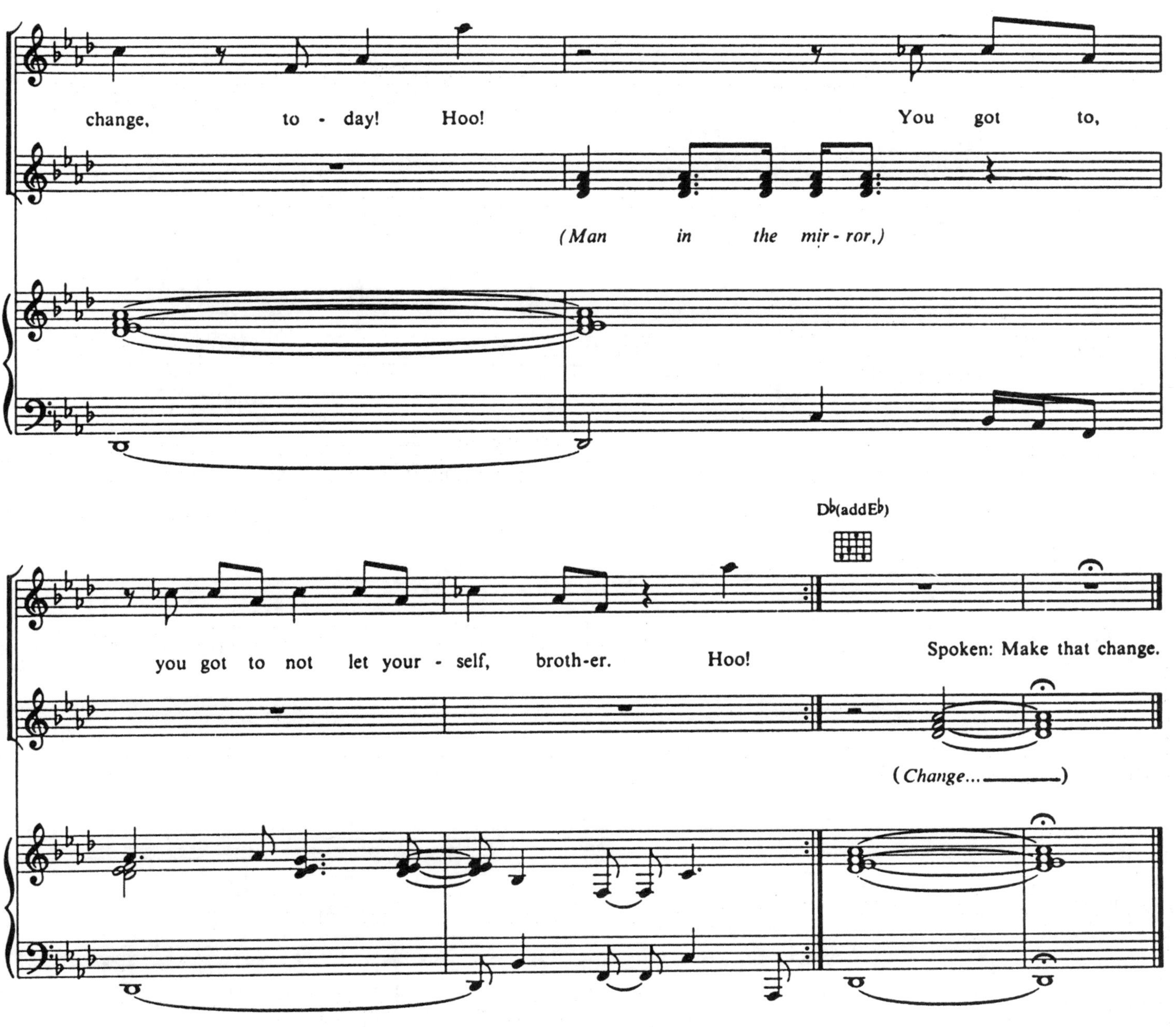

Additional Lyrics for repeat:
(Yeah!-Make that change)
You know-I've got to get
that man, that man...
(Man in the mirror)
You've got to
You've got to move! Come
on! Come on!
You got to...
Stand up! Stand up!
Stand up!
(Yeah!-Make that change)
Stand up and lift
yourself, now!
(Man in the mirror)
Hoo! Hoo! Hoo!
Aaow!
(Yeah!-Make that change)
Gonna make that change...
come on!
You know it!
You know it!
You know it!
You know...
(Change...)
Make that change.

THE LIVING YEARS

By
MIKE RUTHERFORD
and B.A. ROBERTSON

Moderately
Ab
4fr.
mf
Gm
3fr.
Bbm
Eb
Ab
4fr.
Verse:
Ab
4fr.
Dbmaj7
4fr.
1. Ev - ery gen - er - a - tion
blames the one be - fore,
(2.) Crum - pled bits of pa - per
filled with im - per - fect thought
3,4. See additional lyrics

Ab
4fr.
and all of their frus - tra - tions come
stilt - ed con - ver - sa - tions I'm a -
Dbmaj7
4fr.
Gb
beat - ing on your door. I know that I'm a pris - 'ner to all my
fraid that's all we've got. You say you just don't see it, he
Bbm
fath - er held so dear, I know that I'm a hos - tage to all his hopes and fears. I just wish
says it's per - fect sense, you just can't get a - gree - ment in this pres - ent tense. We all talk
Eb7sus4
Db/Eb
Eb
Ab
4fr.
To Coda
I could have told him in the liv - ing years.
a dif - 'rent lan - guage, talk - ing in de - fence.

1.
2. 3. 4.
Chorus:
A♭
4fr.
2. Oh,
Say it loud,
D♭
4fr.
E♭
say it clear,
you can lis - ten as
A♭
4fr.
well as you hear.
It's too late
D♭
4fr.
E♭
when we die
to ad - mit we don't

Additional Lyrics

Verse 3:
So we open up a quarrel
Between the present and the past.
We only sacrifice the future
It's the bitterness that lasts.
So don't yield to the fortunes
You sometimes see as fate.
It may have a new perspective
On a different day.
And if you don't give up,
And don't give in
You may just be OK.

Chorus:

Verse 4:
I wasn't there that morning
When my father passed away.
I didn't get to tell him
All the things I had to say.
I think I caught his spirit
Later that same year.
I'm sure I heard his echo
In my baby's new born tears.
I just wish I could have told him
In the living years.

Chorus:

LOVE CHANGES (EVERYTHING)

Words and Music by
DENNIS MORGAN, SIMON CLIMIE
and ROB FISHER

Bridge I:

Gm F/A B♭

mf

I felt the strang - est feel - ing; like a rag - ing
I won - dered, was I des - tined to spend my

Dm Gm F/A

fire it burned. She left; I cried for weeks, and
life a - lone? Ah, girl, you an - swered my ques-tion;

B♭ Gm7/C

I can't for - get her and the les-sons that I learned
this time it's work - ing. You've giv-en me new hope.

cresc.

Chorus:

F

f

Love chang - es,

Dm

chang - es ev - ery - thing. Love makes you fly. It can break your wings.

Dm
changes everything. Love makes the rules from fools to kings;
To Coda
Gm7
F/A
Bb
Gm7/C
love changes,
1.
F
love changes everything.
dim.
mf
Dm7
To Next Strain
2.3. etc.
Repeat and fade
dim.
love changes.
Verse:
C
F
mp
2. Then the years went rollin' by; I grew up and moved away;

C/E Dm C

— had to earn — my pay. Found an-oth-er lov - er then, — but — my

F C/E Dm7

D.S. 𝄋 *al Coda*

heart is sad – to say — it on - ly end - ed up — the same — way.

cresc.

⊕ *Coda*

F

love chang - es ev - ery-thing.

dim.

Bridge II:

Gm7

mf

F/A B♭ Dm Gm7

I've seen the way —

F/A B♭ Gm7/C

D.S.S. 𝄋𝄋

— love shakes – ya, makes — ya, breaks – ya; it's got a pow-er all its own.

cresc.

MANEATER

Words by SARA ALLEN,
DARYL HALL and JOHN OATES

Music by
DARYL HALL and JOHN OATES

D
A/C#
C
many have paid to see what you think you're getting for free the woman is wild, a she-cat tamed by the
wouldn't if I were you I know what she can do, she's deadly man she could really
B
Em7
A
A#dim
purr of a jaguar. Money's the matter. If you're in it for love, you ain't gonna get too
rip your world apart. Mind over matter oo the beauty is there, but a beast is in the
Bm
A/B
B
Bm
A
G
far.
heart.
Oh, here she comes, watch out boy, she'll chew you up. Oh, here she comes, she's a Man-
F#
Bm
A
Em7
-eat-er. Oh, here she comes, watch out boy, she'll chew you up. Oh, here she comes, she a Man-
G
A
Bm
Bm
Bm
A
-eat-er. (Synth) I (Sax solo) (echo)

G
A
Bm
A
G
A
Bm
A
G
A
Bm
A
Em7
F#7
Bm
A
G
F#
Oh, here she comes, watch out boy, she'll chew you up. Oh, here she comes, she's a Man - eat - er.
Bm
A
Em7
G
A
Repeat and Fade
Oh, here she comes, watch out boy, she'll chew you up. Oh, here she comes, she's a Man - eat - er.

ONE IN A MILLION YOU

Slowly ♩ = 69
Words and Music by
SAM DEES
Eb
(F Bass)
mp
pp
Bbmaj7
1.
2. NC
8va
gliss. on black keys
gliss.
gliss.
Bb
Bbmaj9
1. Love had played it's games on me so long, I start - ed to
2. lone - ly man with emp - ty arms to fill, then I found
Fm9
(Bb Bass)
Ab
(C Bass)
4th fret
Bb7
(D Bass)
Ebmaj7
be - lieve I'd nev - er find an - y - one. Doubt had tried
a piece of hap - pi - ness to call my own. Now life

Ab7 (add 13)
Ab7
Bb (F Bass)
Cm7
to con-vince_me to give in, said you_can't win._
is worth liv - in' a - gain, for to love you, to me,_ is to
1.
F11
Bb
Bbmaj9
But one day the sun_ came_ a-shin - in' through._ The
Fm9 (Bb Bass)
Ab (C Bass) 4th fret
Bb7 (D Bass)
Ebmaj7
Ab7 (add 13)
Ab7
rain had stopped_ and the skies_ were blue,_ and oh, what a rev-e-la-
to next strain
Bb (F Bass)
F#dim
Gm7
Cm7
Eb (F Bass)
tion to see some-one was say-ing, "I love you" to me._ A

Chorus
Eb (F Bass)
Bb
Bbmaj9
Bb7
Ab
4th fret
(C Bass)
Bb7
(D Bass)
live. A one in a mil-lion, chance of a
Ebmaj7
(add 13)
Ab7
Ab7
Bb
(F Bass)
Cm7
Dm7
life-time, and life, showed com - pas-sion and sent to me a
Ebmaj7
F11
Bb
Bb7
(Ab Bass)
Eb
stroke of love called you; a one in a mil-lion you.
Ab7
(add 13)
Ab7
D.S.
Eb(F Bass)
Ab7
(add 13)
Ab7
Bb
(add 2)
2. I was a A A one in a mil-lion you.
pp

MY LOVE

Words and Music by
LIONEL RICHIE

C(2)
C/D
G(2)
D♭(2)
D♭/E♭
A♭(2)
But I sho' need you by my side My love,
Chorus
G
D/G
C
C/D
A♭
E♭/A♭
D♭
D♭/E♭
f
just think - in' a - bout you ba - by Just
G
D/G
C(2)
C/D
A♭
E♭/A♭
D♭(2)
D♭/E♭
blows my mind My love,
G
D/G
C
C/D
A♭
E♭/A♭
D♭
D♭/E♭
just think - in' a - bout you ba - by Just

G
D/G
C(2)
C/D
A♭
E♭/A♭
D♭(2)
D♭/E♭
blows my mind
all
the
G
A♭
time
dim.
G
7fr.
D6/F♯
5fr.
Em7
Bm/D
A♭
E♭6/G
Fm7
Cm/E♭
p
Life with me I know for
sure it ain't been eas - y
C(2)
C/D
G(2)
D♭(2)
D♭/E♭
A♭(2)
But you stayed with me an - y - way

G
D6/F♮
Em7
7fr.
5fr.
A♭
E♭6/G
Fm7
And e - ven though you ain't gon - na lose too much by leav - ing
C(2)
C/D
G
7fr.
D♭(2)
D♭/E♭
A♭
I'm so glad you stayed My love,
G
D/G
C
C/D
G
D/G
A♭
E♭/A♭
D♭
D♭/E♭
A♭
E♭/A♭
just think - in' a - bout you ba - by Just blows my mind
C(2)
C/D
G
D/G
C
C/D
D♭(2)
D♭/E♭
A♭
E♭/A♭
D♭
D♭/E♭
My love, just think - in' a - bout you ba - by Just

G
D/G
C(2)
C/D
To Coda
G
Ab
Eb/Ab
Db(2)
Db/Eb
Ab
blows my mind ___ all the time
p cresc.
C
C/D
G
Db
Db/Eb
Ab
You've been my friend and you've been my lov - er, oh Lawd
f
C
C/D
G
Db
Db/Eb
Ab
Hon - ey, you're ev - 'ry - thing ___ I need.___
C
C/D
G
Bm/F♯
Bø7/F
Db
Db/Eb
Ab
Cm/G
Cø7/Gb
You've made my love so strong, now I know where I be - long

E7
Am7
Bm7
Cmaj7
3fr.
F7
B♭m7
Cm7
D♭maj7
3
Oh girl, you'll nev - er have to wor - ry
Oh
Cmaj7/D
7fr.
G(2)
Dm/G
D♭maj7/E♭
A♭(2)
E♭m/A♭
ba - by, an - y - more,
an - y -
C(2)
Cm(2)
D♭(2)
D♭m(2)
D.S. al Coda
more
My love,
f sub.
Coda
G
D/G
C(2)
C/D
G
A♭
E♭/A♭
D♭(2)
D♭/E♭
A♭
time
Oh
yeah
rall.

ON THE WINGS OF LOVE

Words by
JEFFREY OSBORNE

Music by
PETER SCHLESS

Em
Em(#7)
G/D
C#m7-5
And I'm sure that you're an an - gel in dis - guise.
Am7
G/B
1.
Am7/D
D(add9)
To next strain
Come take my hand and to - geth - er we will ride.
cresc.
2.
Am7/D
D
D(add9)
Chorus:
G
G/B
you would come with me.
On the wings of love, up and a - bove
cresc.
f
Cmaj7
C/D
D
Em
Em(#7)
Em7/B
the clouds; the on - ly way to fly is

Em7/A
Am7/D
G
G/B
on the wings of love.
On the wings of love,
only the two
Cmaj7
C/D
D
Em
Em(♯7)
G/D
of us to-geth - er fly - ing high;
G/A
A7
Am7/D
1. G(add9)
D.S.
fly - ing high up - on the wings of love.
f
2. G(add9)
C
Yes, you be - long to me,
mf

G/B
Am
Am/D
and I'm yours ex - clu - sive - ly. And right now we live and
Am/G
G
F/G
G
C
breathe to - geth - er. In - sep - 'ra - ble it seems,
G/B
C
G/B
we're flow - ing like a stream run - ning free trav - el - ing
Am7
Am7/D
Bbm7/Eb
on the wings of love.
cresc.

Ab
Ab/C
Dbmaj7
Db/Eb
Eb
On the wings of love, up and a - bove the clouds; the on - ly way to fly
Fm
Fm(#7)
Fm7/C
Ab/Bb
Bb7
Bbm7/Eb
Eb7
is on the wings of love.
Ab
Ab/C
Dbmaj7
Db/Eb
Eb
On the wings of love, on - ly the two of us to - geth - er fly - ing high;
1.
Fm
Fm(#7)
Fm7/C
Ab/Bb
Bb7
Bbm7/Eb
Eb7
to - geth - er fly - ing high.

Verse 2:
You look at me and I begin to melt
Just like the snow, when a ray of sun is felt.
And I'm crazy 'bout you, baby, can't you see?
I'd be so delighted if you would come with me.
(To Chorus:)

ONE MORE NIGHT

Words and Music by
PHIL COLLINS

Eb
Ab
4fr.
Eb/Bb
Fm7
3
let you know, let you know how I feel.
wast - ing time, just star - ing at the phone.
feel the same. And I know it's on - ly words.

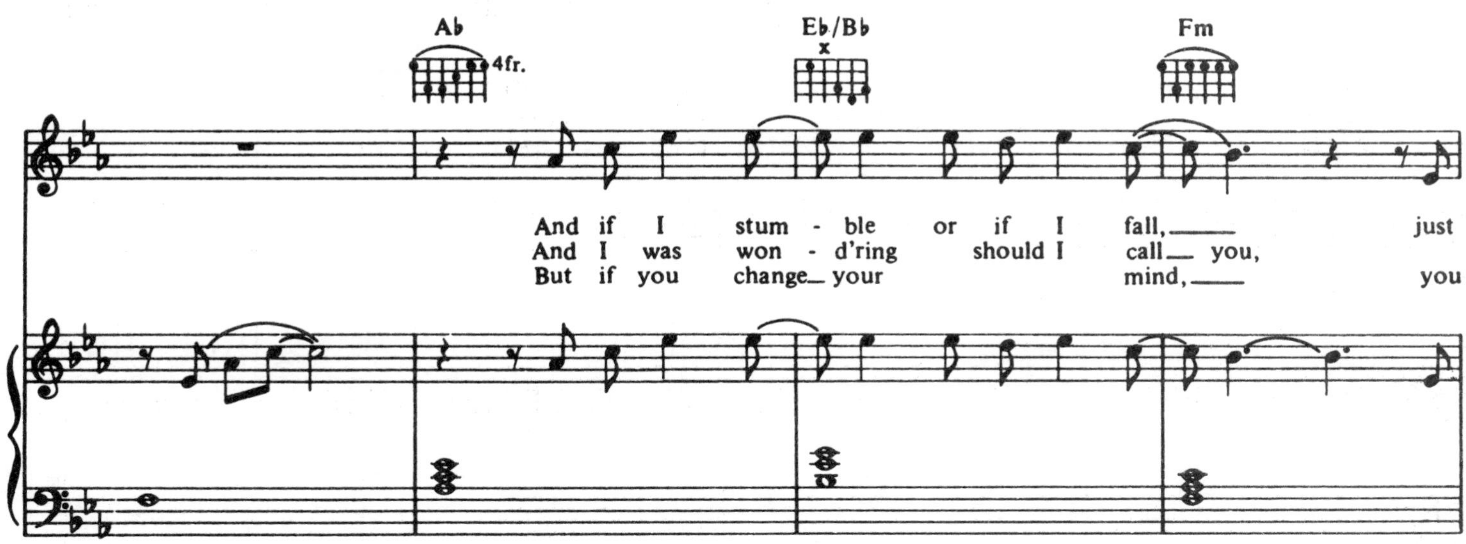
Ab
4fr.
Eb/Bb
Fm
And if I stum - ble or if I fall, just
And I was won - d'ring should I call you,
But if you change your mind, you

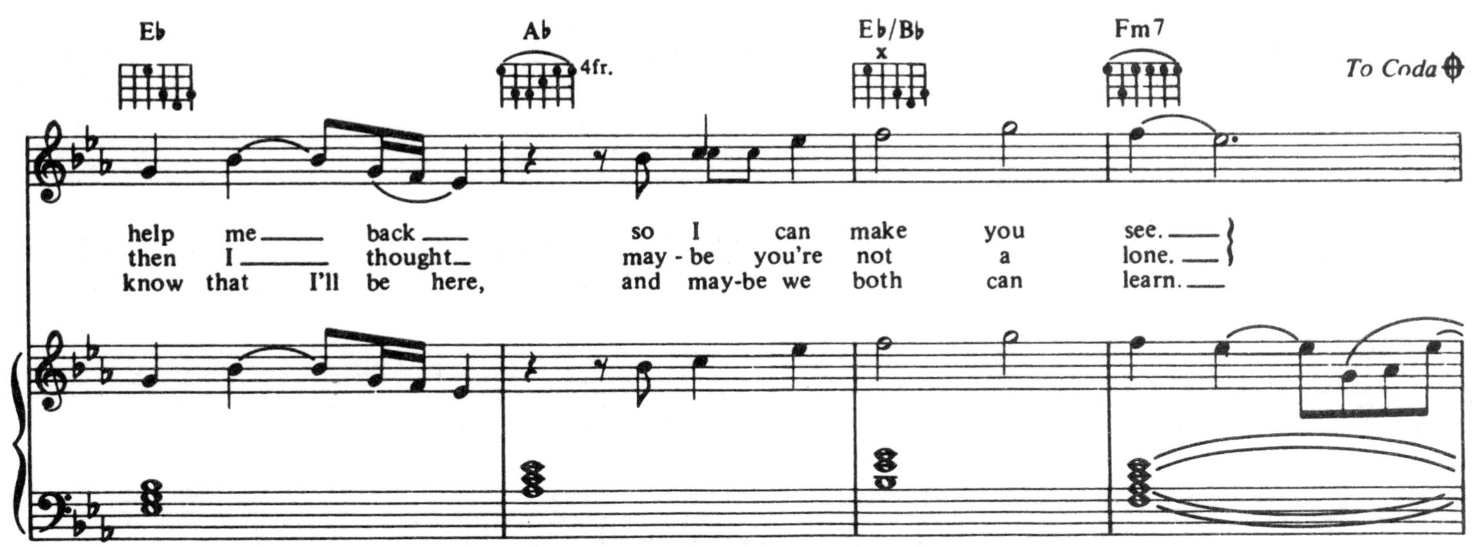
Eb
Ab
4fr.
Eb/Bb
Fm7
To Coda
help me back so I can make you see.
then I thought may - be you're not a lone.
know that I'll be here, and may-be we both can learn.

Bb Eb Bb Bb/D Eb

Please_ give me one more night.__ Give me one more night,_

Bb Eb Fm7 Fm9 Bb

__ one more night,__ 'cause I can't_ wait for-ev - er.

Eb Bb Bb/D Eb

Give me just one more night,__ just one more night,_

Fm7
Fm9
B♭
1.
2.
wait for - ev - er.
Give me
E♭
B♭
B♭/D
E♭
one more night. Give me just one more night,
B♭
E♭
one more night 'cause I
Fm7
Fm9
B♭
Cm7
3fr.
E♭/D♭
can't wait for - ev - er.
Like a riv -

Cm7
3fr.
Db/Eb
er to the sea,
I will al - ways be with
Cm7
3fr.
Eb/Db
Cm7
3fr.
Eb/Db
you.
And if you sail a - way,
I will fol -
Bb
Eb
low you.
Give me one more night.
Bb
Bb/D
Eb
Give me just one more night,
oh,

Bb
Eb
Fm7
Fm9
Bb
one more night, 'cause I can't wait for-ev - er.
Coda
Bb
Eb
Give me just a one more night. Give me just a
Bb
Bb/D
Eb
Bb
Eb
one more night, one more night
Fm7
Fm9
Bb
1.
2.
D.S. 𝄋𝄋 (instrumental) and fade
'cause I can't wait for-ev - er. Give me just a

OPEN ARMS

Words and Music by
STEVE PERRY and JONATHAN CAIN

Slowly
D
A/C♯
G/B
p
expressively
sim.
Bm
A
G
Verse:
D
A/C♯
G/B
Bm
1. Ly - ing be - side you, here in the dark; feel - ing your
2. Soft - ly you whis - per, you're so sin - cere. How could our
3.4. (see additional lyrics)
mp
A
G
1.3.
2.4.
heart beat with mine.
love be so blind?
1. We
2. (see additional lyrics)
mf

Em
Bm
A/C♯
D
sailed on___ to- geth - er; we drift- ed__ a - part; and here you
A
G
A/G
G
are by my__ side.____ So, now I
Chorus:
D
F♯m
come_______ to you_______ with o - pen arms;____
here_______ I am_______ with o - pen arms;____
f
G
1.3. C
noth - ing_____ to hide, be - lieve what I say._______ So,
hop - ing_____ you see what your

Verse 3:
Living without you; living alone,
This empty house seems so cold.

Verse 4:
Wanting to hold you, wanting you near;
How much I wanted you home.

Bridge:
But now that you've come back;
Turned night into day;
I need you to stay.
(Chorus)

SAY YOU, SAY ME

Words and Music by
LIONEL RICHIE

Fm
Ab/Eb
4fr.
Cm/Eb
4fr.
Db
4fr.
Db/Eb
6fr.
Ab
4fr.
Ab/Eb
4fr.
Say it to-geth - er, nat-'ral-ly.
Ab
4fr.
Eb/G
Fm
Ab/Eb
4fr.
Cm
3fr.
I had a dream, I had an awe-some dream:
As we go down life's lone-some high-way, seems the
Bbm
Ab
4fr.
Gb
Eb
6fr.
peo-ple in the park play-in' games in the dark.
hard-est thing to do is to find a friend or two.
Ab
4fr.
Eb/G
Fm
Ab/Eb
4fr.
Cm
3fr.
And what they played was a mas-quer-ade. But from be-
That help-ing hand, some-one who un-der-stands. And when you

B♭m
A♭
4fr.
1. G♭
hind the walls of doubt, a voice was cry - ing out.
feel you've lost your way, you've got
E♭
6fr.
2. G♭
E♭
6fr.
some-one there to say, "I'll show you."
A♭
4fr.
E♭/G
Fm
A♭/E♭
4fr.
Cm
3fr.
D♭
4fr.
D♭/E♭
6fr.
Say you, say me. Say it for al - ways. That's the
A♭
4fr.
E♭/A♭
3fr.
E♭
6fr.
A♭
4fr.
E♭/G
Fm
A♭/E♭
4fr.
Cm
3fr.
To Coda
way it should be. Say you, say me. Say it to - geth-

Faster
Db
Db/Eb
Ab
4fr.
6fr.
4fr.
er, nat - 'ral - ly. So you
Cb
Gb
Db
Ab
4fr.
4fr.
think you know the an - swers. Oh, no. Well, the
Cb
Gb
D
Ebm
5fr.
6fr.
whole world's got ya danc - in', that's right, I'm tell - in' you. It's
Cb
Gb
Db
Ab
4fr.
4fr.
time to start be - liev - in'. oh, yes. Be -

Tempo I
C♭
(♩.=♩)
D♭
4fr.
E♭
6fr.
D.S. al Coda
lieve in who you are; you are a shin - ing star.
Coda
D♭
4fr.
D♭/E♭
6fr.
A♭
E♭/A♭
3fr.
E♭
6fr.
er. nat - 'ral - ly. Say it to - geth-
D♭
4fr.
A♭/C
B♭m7
D♭/E♭
6fr.
A♭
4fr.
er, nat - 'ral - ly.
rit.

SHOULD'VE KNOWN BETTER

Words and Music by
RICHARD MARX

A/G
G
xooo
Bb/Ab
Ab
A/G
G
xooo
Bb/Ab
Ab
Bm7
A/B
Cm7
Bb/C
Bm7
A/B
Cm7
Bb/C
An - oth - er sleep - less night I can't ex - plain.
There was no risk that I would - n't take,
I can't re - mem - ber if the lies were true.
D/G
A/G
Eb/Ab
Bb/Ab
D/G
A/G
Eb/Ab
Bb/Ab
Some-bod - y said they heard me call your name.
and not a prom - ise that I did - n't make.
It's been a mil - lion years since I touched you.

D/A
A
A/G
G
E♭/B♭
B♭
B♭/A♭
A♭
The ra - di - o won't let you leave my mind.
All I asked was that you just hold on.
I thought time might help me win this game,
I know it's o - ver but I don't know why.
And now I'm won - der - ing what I did wrong.
but being a - way from you is slow - ly driv - ing me in - sane.
Dsus4
D
Asus4
A
E♭sus4
E♭
B♭sus4
B♭
I should have known bet - ter than to fall in love with

A/G G Em9add4
Bb/Ab Ab Fm9 add4

you. Now love is just a fad - ed mem - o - ry.

Dsus4 D Asus4 A
Ebsus4 Eb Bbsus4 Bb

Should - 've known bet - ter. Now I'm a pris - 'ner to this

A/G G F#m7 Em9 A/E To Coda 1. Em7 G/A
Bb/Ab Ab Gm7 Fm9 Bb/F Fm7 Ab/Bb

pain. And my heart still aches for

Bm7
A/B
Cm7
Bb/C
you.
Ooh.
D/G
A/G
Eb/Ab
Bb/Ab
2. Em7
G/A
G
3fr.
Fm7
Ab/Bb
Ab
aches for you.
I gave you all of my bod - y and

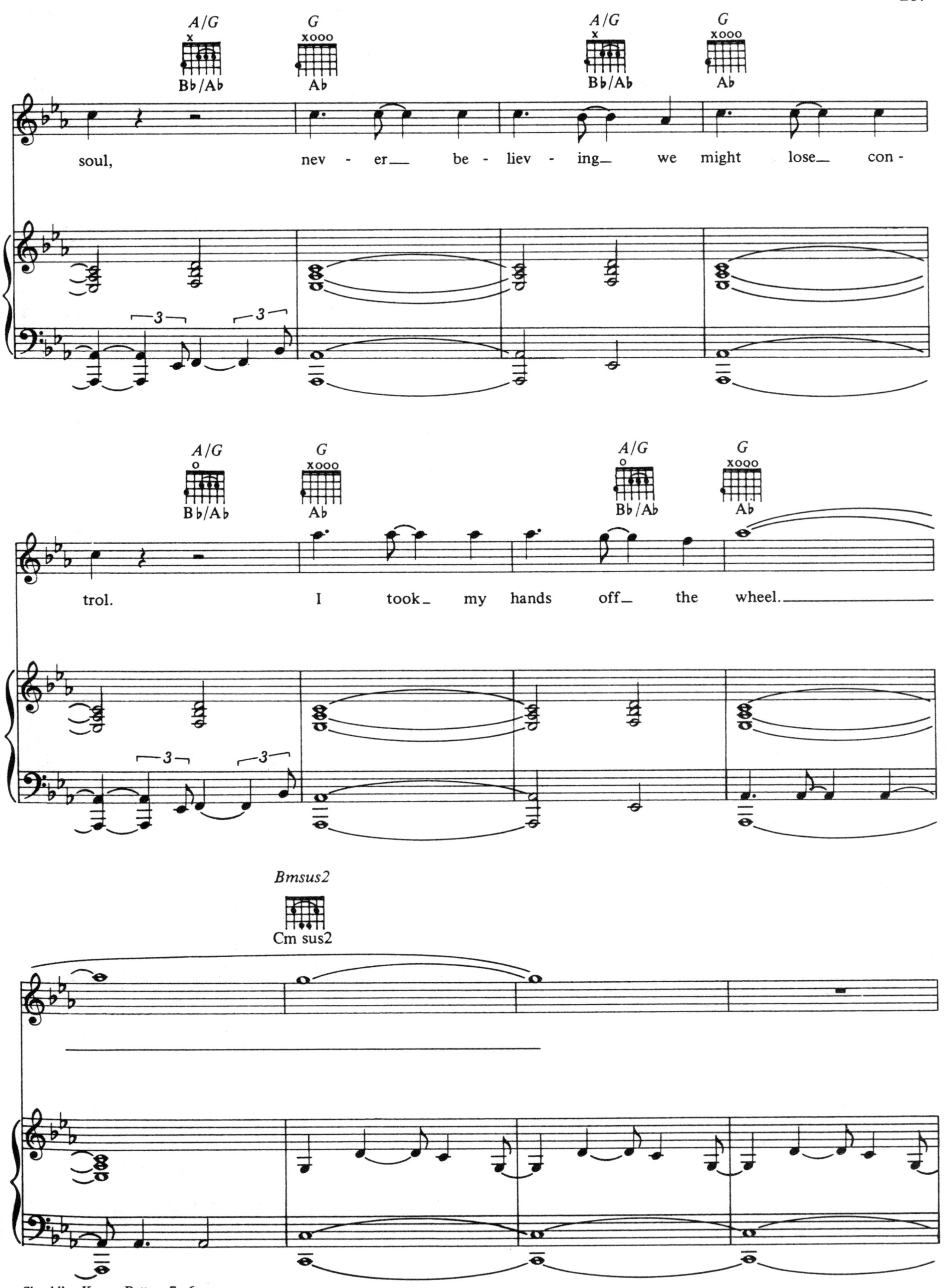
A/G
G
Bb/Ab
Ab
soul, never be - liev - ing we might lose con -
trol. I took my hands off the wheel.
Bmsus2
Cm sus2

Ab maj7 add6
3fr.
Asus4
Bbsus4
Gmaj7-5
2fr.
Abmaj7-5
E6/9
F6/9
A6/9
Bb6/9
D.S. al Coda
Coda
Em7
2fr.
Fm7
G/A
3fr.
Ab/Bb
Dsus4
Ebsus4
D
Eb
D.S. and fade
aches for you. I should have known_bet - ter

SUDDENLY

By
KEITH DIAMOND and
BILLY OCEAN

Suddenly - 3 - 1

Chorus:
A
Bb
Dm7
Ebm7
G
Ab
A
Bb
ly, life has new mean - ing to me. There's
Dm7
Ebm7
G
Ab
To Coda
Cmaj7
Dbmaj7
Fmaj7
Gbmaj7
beaut - y up a - bove; and things we nev - er take no - tice of; you
Esus
Fsus
E/G♯
F/A
1.
Am
Bbm
Am(add9)/G
Bbm(add9)/Ab
Am(add9)/F
Bbm(add9)/Gb
G
Ab
wake up and sud - den - ly you're in love.
Am(add9)
Bbm(add9)
Am(add9)/G
Bbm(add9)/Ab
Am(add9)/F
Bbm(add9)/Gb
G
Ab
D.S.
2.
A
Bb
G
Ab
F
Gb
G/F
Ab/Gb
2. Girl, you're love. Each day

Verse 2:
Girl, you're everything a man could want and more,
One thousand words are not enough
To say what I feel inside,
Holding hands as we walk along the shore
Never felt like this before,
Now you're all I'm living for.

TAKE ME HOME

Words and Music by
PHIL COLLINS

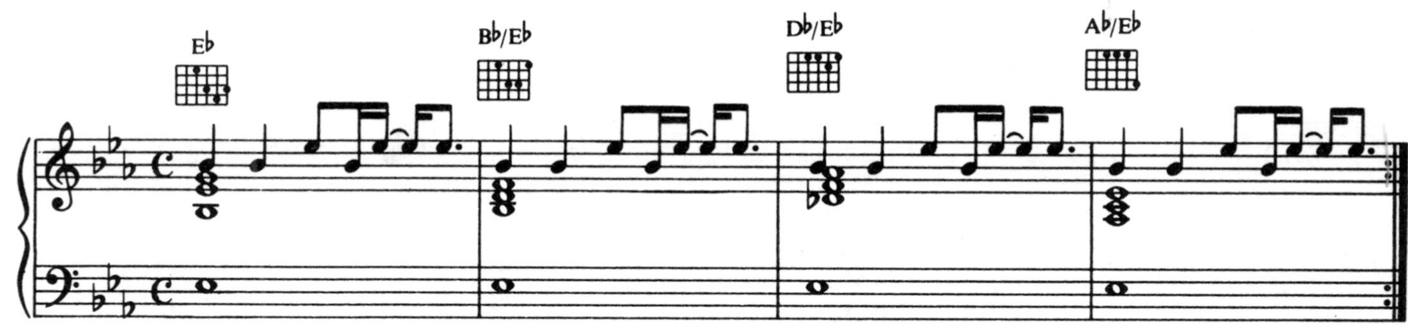
Eb
Bb/Eb
Db/Eb
Ab/Eb

Eb
Bb/Eb
Db/Eb
Take that look of_ wor - ry, I'm an or - di - na - ry man_
Seems so long I've_ been wait-ing still don't know_ what for_
Take that look of_ wor - ry mine's an or - di - na - ry life_

Ab/Eb
Eb
Bb/Eb
they_ don't tell_ me_ no - thing so I
there's no point_ es - cap - ing I don't
work - ing when_ it's_ day - light and

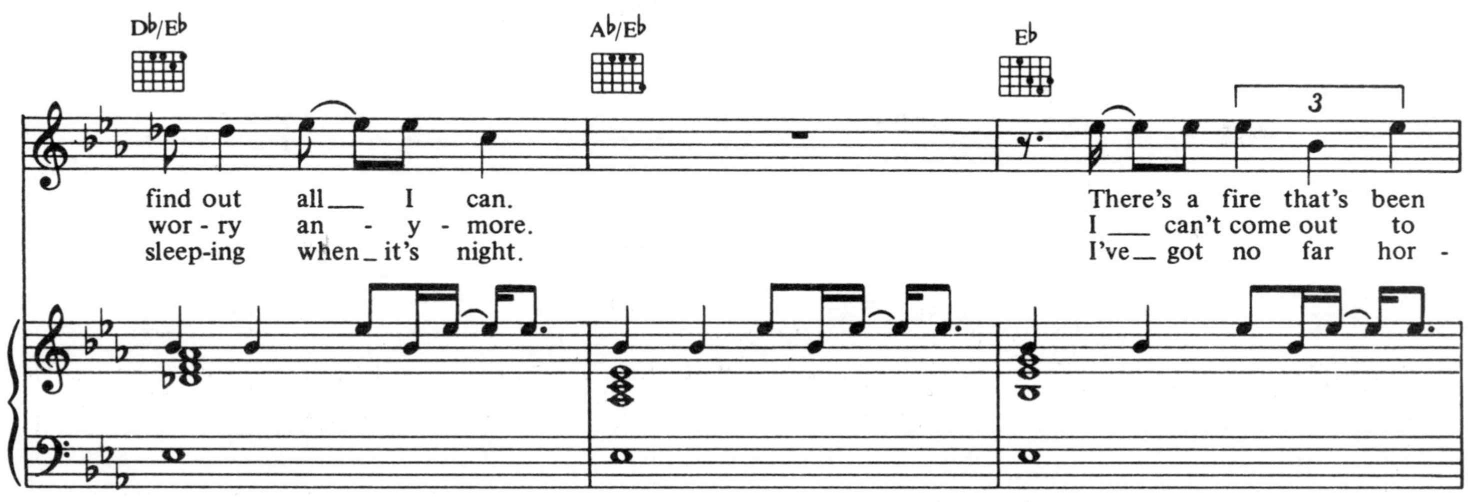
Db/Eb
Ab/Eb
Eb
3
find out all___ I can. There's a fire that's been
wor - ry an - y - more. I ___ can't come out to
sleep-ing when _ it's night. I've _ got no far hor -

Bb/Eb
Db/Eb
Ab/Eb
burn - ing right out - side__ my________ door._____
find you I don't like to go___ out - side _____
iz - ons I don't wish up - on___ a ________ star._____

Eb
Bb/Eb
Db/Eb
3
I _ can't see but I feel it and it helps to keep_ me warm.
They can turn off my feel-ings like they're turn - ing off _ the light.
They don't think that I lis - ten oh but I know who _ they are._

Ab/Eb
Abadd9/Eb
Ab/Eb
So__
But__
And__
I,
I
don't
Eb
Abadd9/Eb
mind,
no__
I,
Ab/Eb
Eb
1
I
don't__
mind.__
2
Dbadd9/Eb
Db/Eb
oh__
I,
I
don't
mind.__
continue pattern (opt.)

E♭
D♭add9/E♭
No I,
D♭/E♭
E♭
I don't mind. So
E♭
A♭/E♭
take, take me home
E♭
'cause I don't re - mem - ber. Take, take me

Ab/Eb
Eb
home 'cause I don't re - mem - ber.
Ab/Eb
To Coda
Bb/Eb
Take, take me home oh no
Fm
Eb/G
Db/Ab
3
3
'cause I've been a prison-er all my life and I can
Fm
D.%. al Coda
say to you,
CODA
'cause I don't re - mem-

E♭
A♭/E♭
ber, take, take me home
B♭/E♭
Fm
E♭/G
oh no, 'cause I've been a prison-er all my life
D♭/A♭
Fm
E♭
and I can say to you, but I don't re-mem - ber
A♭/E♭
Repeat to Fade
take, take me home 'cause I don't re-mem-

From the Vestron Motion Picture "DIRTY DANCING"

(I'VE HAD) THE TIME OF MY LIFE

Words and Music by
FRANKE PREVITE, DONALD MARKOWITZ
and JOHN DeNICOLA

Moderately ♩ = 104

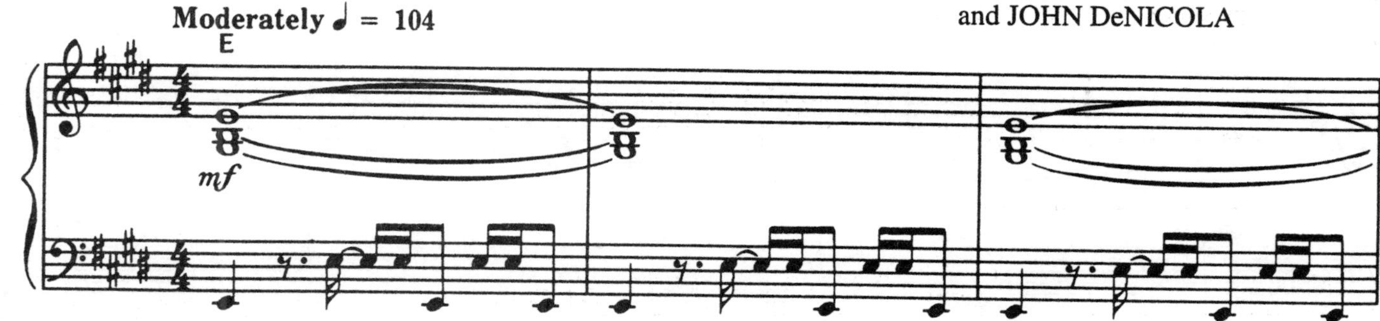

*sung on all repeats

D E

life; no, I nev - er felt this way be - fore. Yes I
life, and I've searched through ev - 'ry o - pen door till I've

C♯m D 1.

swear it's the truth, and I owe it all to you.
found the truth,

E D/E E *D.S.* 𝄋

mf

2. With my

2.4.5. *etc.* *Repeat ad lib. and fade* 3. E

owe it all to you. Be-cause owe it all to you.

mf

D/E F♯7sus B7sus E

Intr. solo ad lib. . . .

C♯m D

(end solo)

f

E C♯m

I've had the time of my

p

D E

life, and I nev - er felt this way be - fore. Yes, I

D.S.S. 𝄋𝄋

C♯m D E D/F♯ E/G♯ D/A B7sus

swear it's the truth, and I owe it all to you.

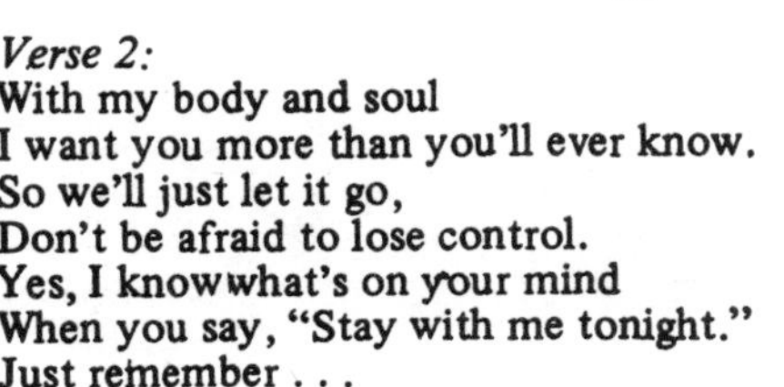
Verse 2:
With my body and soul
I want you more than you'll ever know.
So we'll just let it go,
Don't be afraid to lose control.
Yes, I knowwhat's on your mind
When you say, "Stay with me tonight."
Just remember . . .

TONIGHT I CELEBRATE MY LOVE

Words and Music by
MICHAEL MASSER and GERRY GOFFIN

Eb
Cm7
Fm7
Ab/Bb
Ab
night no one's gon - na find us, we'll leave the world be -
night our spir - its will be climb - ing to a sky lit up with
mf
Gm7
Cm9
1.
Fm7
Ab/Bb
hind us, when I make love to you. 2. To -
dia - monds when I make
mp
2.
Abmaj7
Ab/Bb
Eb
Bb/Eb
love to you to - night.
Ab/Eb
To next strain
3.
Abmaj7
Ab/Bb
Bb
To - love to you. To -

Chorus:
Abmaj7
Gm7
Db/Eb
Eb7
night I cel - e - brate my love for you and the
f
Abmaj7
Gm7
Db/Eb
Eb7
mid - night sun is gon - na come shin - ing through. To -
Abmaj7
Gm7
Fm7
Gm7
Cm7
night there'll be no dis - tance be - tween us. What I want
Abmaj7
Abm(#7)
most to do is to get close to you to -
decresc.

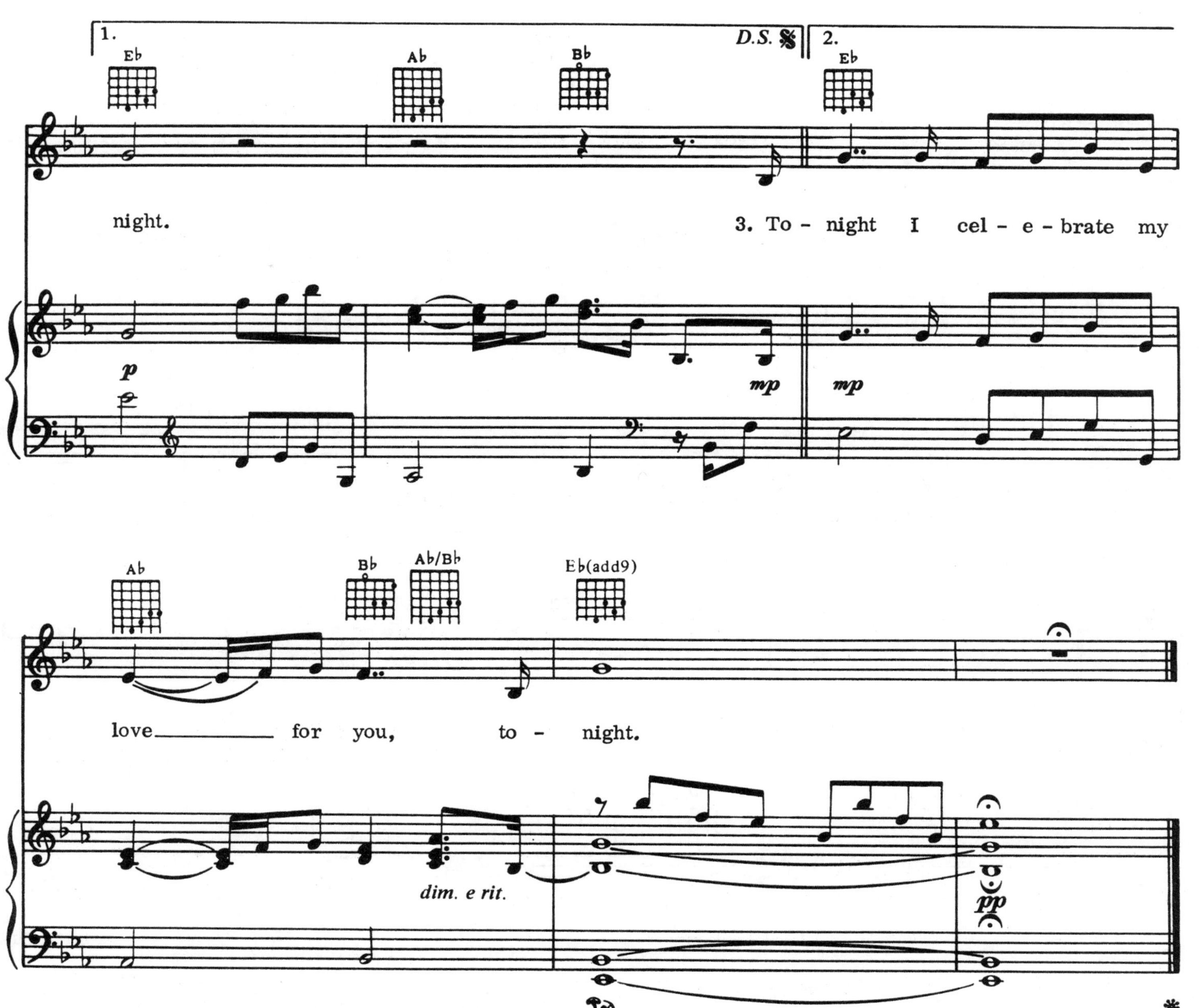

Verse 3:
Tonight I celebrate my love for you,
And soon this old world will seem brand new.
Tonight we will both discover
How friends turn into lovers,
When I make love to you.
(To Chorus:)

Paramount Pictures Presents A Lorimar-Martin Elfand Production-A Taylor Hackford Film
"AN OFFICER AND A GENTLEMAN"

UP WHERE WE BELONG

Words by
WILL JENNINGS

Music by
JACK NITZSCHE and BUFFY SAINTE-MARIE

Em7
A
road is long. There are
cresc.
D
D/F♯
G
G/B
C
D/C
mountains in our way, but we climb a step ev-'ry
mp
Chorus:
A
G/A
A
D
D/F♯
G
Bm
day. Love lift us up where we be-long, where the
cresc.
f
Em
D/F♯
C
G
A
D
D/F♯
ea-gles cry on a moun-tain high. Love lift us up where we be-long,

G
Bm
Em
D/F♯
far from the world we know; up where the
1.
F♯/A♯
Bm
Gm
D
G/D
Gm/D
clear winds blow.
3
decresc.
2.
G/A
A
F
C/E
E♭
B♭/D
clear winds blow. Time goes by, no time to cry,
decresc.
mp
D♭
A♭/C
B♭
Fm7/B♭
E♭
life's you and I, a - live, to - day.
cresc. poco a poco
f

Verse 2:
Some hang on to "used-to-be",
Live their lives looking behind.
All we have is here and now;
All our life, out there to find.
The road is long.
There are mountains in our way,
But we climb them a step every day.

WAITING FOR A STAR TO FALL

Lyrics and Music by
GEORGE MERRILL and
SHANNON RUBICAM

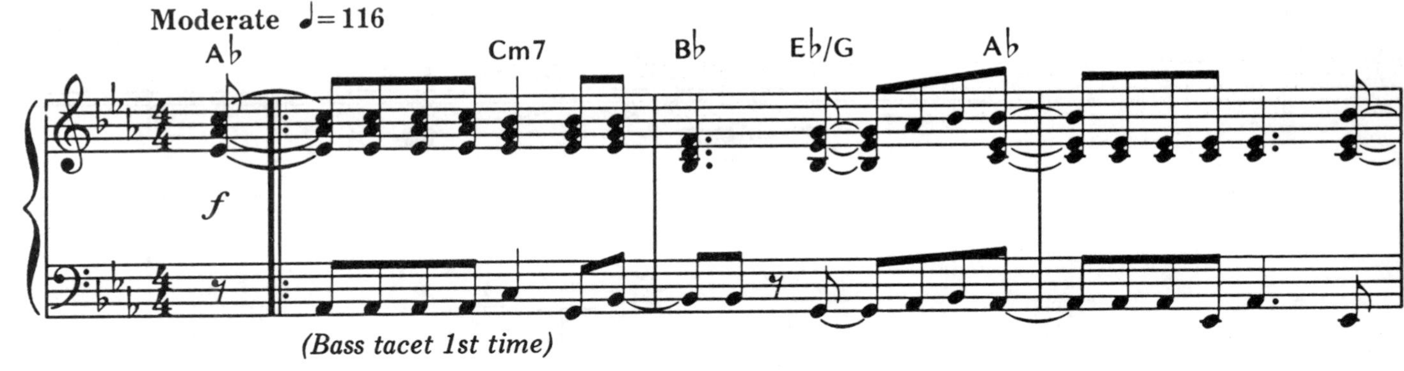
Moderate ♩=116
A♭
Cm7
B♭
E♭/G
A♭
f
(Bass tacet 1st time)

B♭
1.

2.
Verse:
A♭/E♭
E♭
Fm/E♭
E♭
E♭/G
dim.
mp
1. I hear your name whis-pered on the wind, it's a sound
2. I've learned to feel what I can - not see, but with you

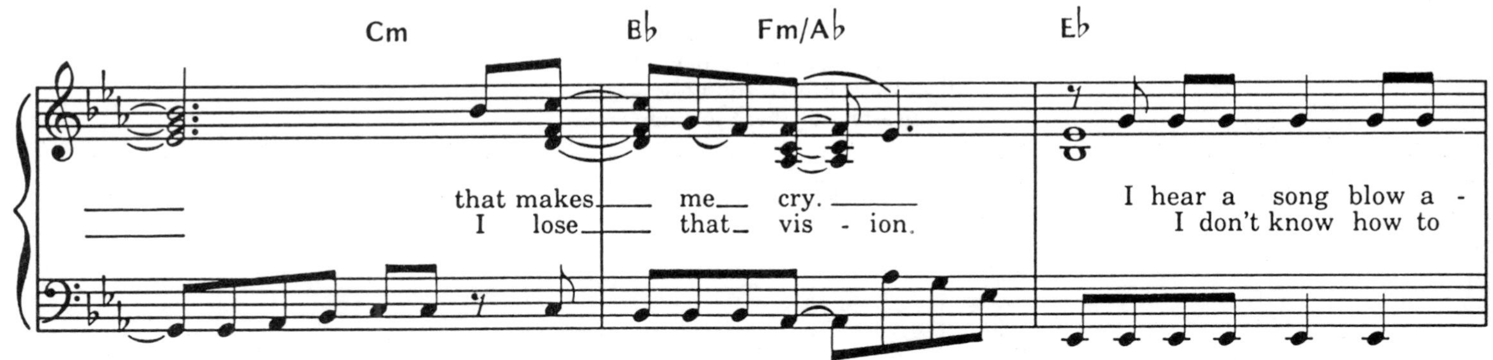
Cm
B♭
Fm/A♭
E♭
that makes me cry.
I lose that vis - ion.
I hear a song blow a -
I don't know how to

Fm/Eb
Eb
Eb/G
Cm
Bb
Fm/Ab
gain and a - gain through my mind, and I don't know why.
dream your dream so I'm all caught up in su - per - sti - tion.

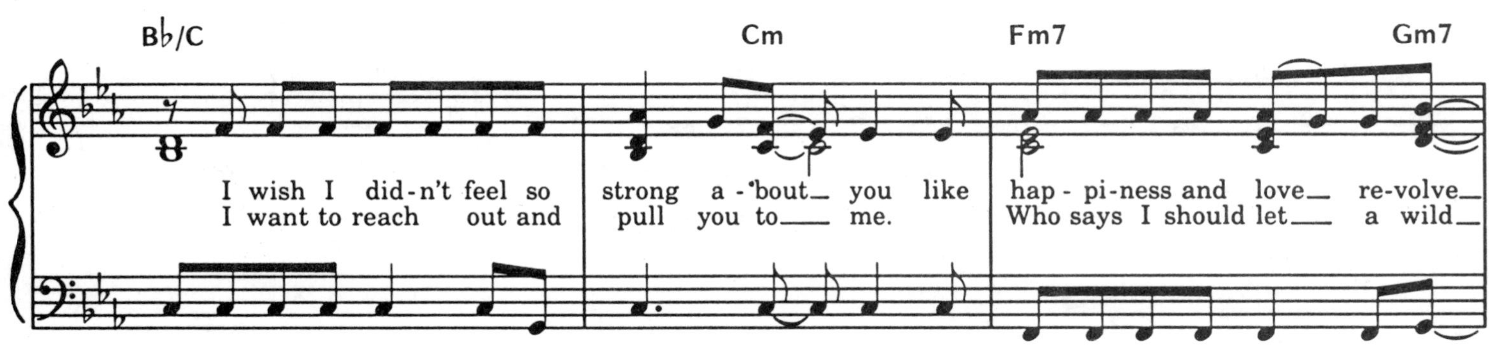
Bb/C
Cm
Fm7
Gm7
I wish I did - n't feel so strong a - 'bout you like hap - pi - ness and love re - volve
I want to reach out and pull you to me. Who says I should let a wild

Bb
Cm
Bb
Ab
Bb
a - round you.
one go free?
Try - ing to catch your heart is like try -

Cm
Bb
Ab
Fm7
- ing to catch a star.
So man - y peo - ple love
But I can't love you this

Bbsus
Ab
you ba - by,
much ba - by,
that must be what you are.
and love you from this far.
cresc.
Wait-
f
Chorus:
Cm
Bb
Eb/G
Ab
- ing for a star to fall and car - ry your heart in - to my arms, that's
Bb
Ab
where you be-long, in my arms ba - by, yeah.
Wait -
Cm
Bb
Eb/G
Ab
- ing for a star to fall and car - ry your heart in - to my arms, that's
1.
D.S.
Bb
Ab/Eb
Eb
where you be-long, in my arms ba - by, yeah.
dim.
mp

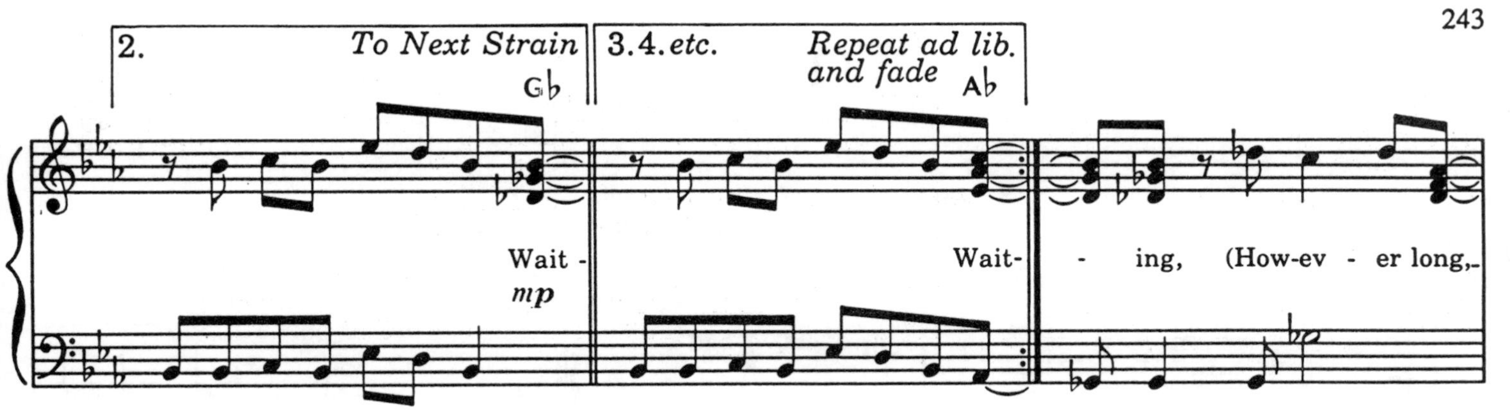
2.
To Next Strain
3.4.etc.
Repeat ad lib. and fade
G♭
A♭
Wait -
mp
Wait-
- ing, (How-ev - er long,-

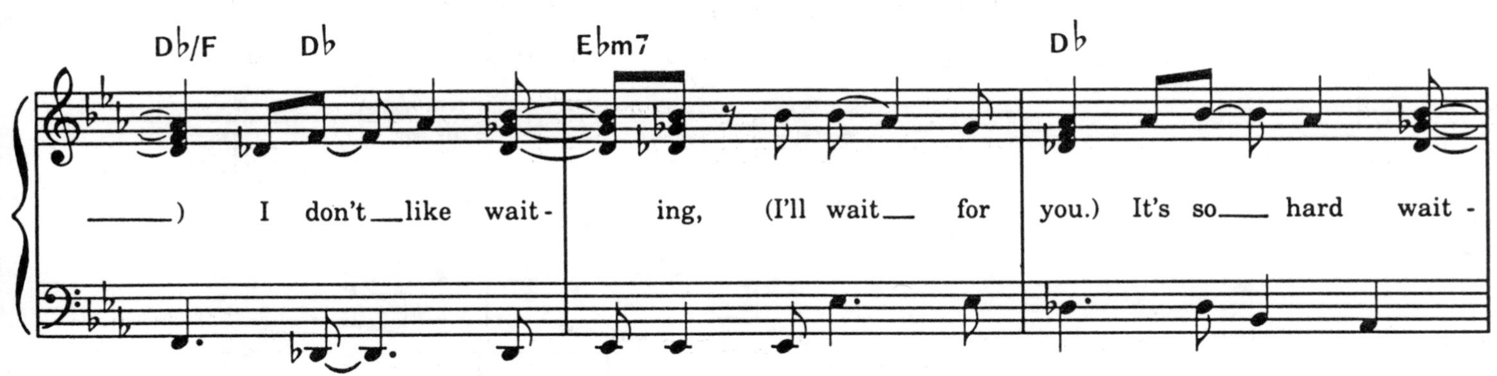
D♭/F
D♭
E♭m7
D♭
) I don't like wait -
ing, (I'll wait for
you.) It's so hard wait -

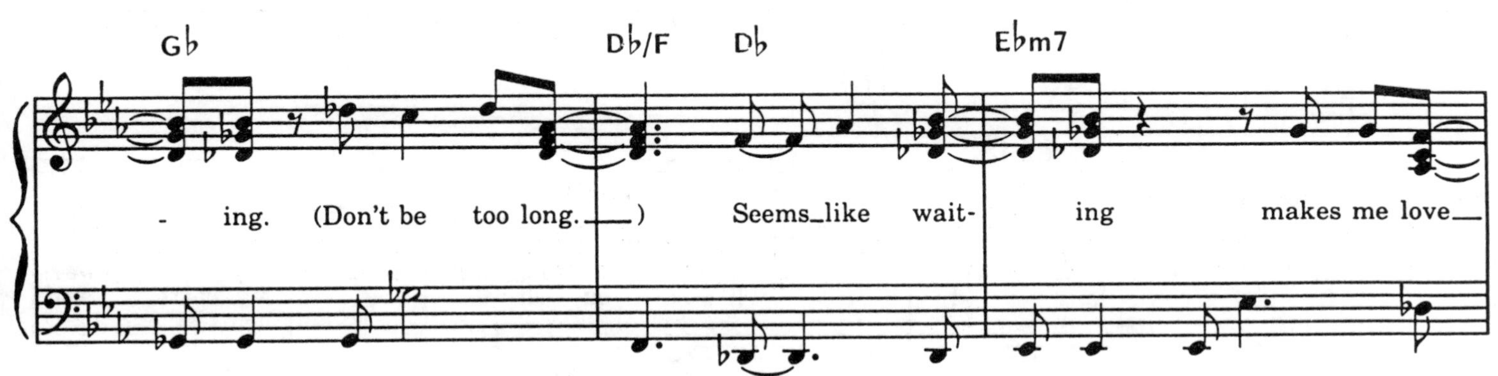
G♭
D♭/F
D♭
E♭m7
- ing. (Don't be too long.)
Seems like wait-
ing makes me love

D.S.S.
A♭/C
B♭/D
B♭
C
E♭
B♭
A♭
you e - ven
more.
Wait -
cresc.
f

TRULY

Words and Music by
LIONEL RICHIE

Fmaj7
Em7
Fmaj7
Em7
Gbmaj7
Fm7
Gbmaj7
Fm7
3
lov - er
And I know if
you real - ly
care I will
near me
And I feel with
you in my
arms This
1.
2.
Dm7
G7/4
G
G4
G
Dm7
G7/4
G
G4
G
Ebm7
Ab7/4
Ab
Ab4
Ab
Ebm7
Ab7/4
Ab
Ab4
Ab
al - ways
be
there
love will last
for - ev - er Be-cause I'm
cresc.
C(2)
C7
Fmaj7
Db(2)
Db7
Gbmaj7
3
tru - ly,
Tru - ly in
love
with you, Girl
F/G
C(2)
C7
Gb/Ab
Db(2)
Db7
3
3
I'm
tru - ly,
head o - ver

Fmaj7
Gbmaj7
F/G
Gb/Ab
C(2)
Db(2)
heels with your love I need you
C7
Db7
Fmaj7
Gbmaj7
F/G
Gb/Ab
And with your love I'm free And
C(2)
Db(2)
C7
Db7
F
Gb
C/E
Db/F
Dm7
Ebm7
tru - ly, You know you're all right
Dm7-5
Ebm7-5
C(2)
Db(2)
with me

WHILE YOU SEE A CHANCE

Words by WILL JENNINGS

Music by STEVE WINWOOD

D
A/C♯
Bm7
Em
Stand up in a clear blue morn - ing, un - til you see
A
D
A/C♯
Bm7
what can be; a - lone in a cold day dawn - ing,
Em
A
D
A/D
G/D
are you still free; can you be?
f
A/D
G/D
D
A/D
G/D
D
A/C♯
G/B
G

Em7/A
D
G/B
G
D/A
A
F♯m
D9
G
Gmaj7
Em9
D/A
Gmaj7
When some cold to - mor - row finds you; when some sad old dream re-minds
When there's no one left to leave you; e - ven you don't quite be-lieve
And that old, grey wind is blow - ing; and there's noth-ing left worth know-
mp
D/A
G
E/G♯
you how the end - less road un - winds you;
you; that's when noth - ing can de - ceive you;
ing; and it's time you should be go - ing;
while you see
cresc.

D/A
F#/A#
Bm
a chance, take it; find ro - mance, fake
D/C
Bm
G/B
A7
To Coda
it; be - cause it's all on you.
D
1. to next strain
2. D.S.S. al Coda
Bb
F/Bb
Eb/Bb
Don't you know
F/Bb
Bb
F/Bb
Eb/Bb
by now, no one gives you an - y - thing;

B♭ F/B♭ E♭/B♭ F/E♭ C/G D/A

and don't you won - der how you keep — on mov - ing —

cresc.

A7sus

D.S. 𝄋

— one more day, — your way?

f

D Em/D

1. 2.

— While you

D Em/D

Repeat ad lib and fade

see a chance, — take — it; find ro - mance; while you

WHAT'S LOVE GOT TO DO WITH IT

Words and Music by
GRAHAM LYLE and
TERRY BRITTEN

Verse:
Em7
G♯m7
D/E
F♯/G♯
C
E
D
F♯
must un - der - stand that the touch of your hand makes my
pulse re - act;
that it's on - ly the thrill of
boy meet - ing girl; op - po - sites at - tract.
It's
phys - i - cal,
on - ly log - i - cal,
mp
mf

C
E
D
F♯
you must try to _ ig - nore that it means more than that. Oh, ___
cresc.
Chorus:
Em
G♯m
D
F♯
N.C.
— what's love _ got to do, __ got to do _ with it? What's love __ but a
f
sec - ond hand e - mo - tion? __ What's love __ got to do, _
— got to do _ with it? Who needs _ a heart when _ a

1.
2.
C
D
E
F♯
heart can be bro - ken?_ It
heart can be bro - ken._
F♯m
E
D
Bbm
Ab
Gb
N.C.
instrumental solo ad lib.
G/A
Cb/Db
I've been tak - ing on a
mf

A G/A A
Db Cb/Db Db
new di - rec - tion, but I have to say,
F G/F
A B/A
I've been think - ing 'bout my own pro - tec - tion; it
Em7 A F#m E
Abm7 Db N.C. Bbm Ab
scares me to feel this way. Oh, what's love got to do
bro - ken.
D E F#m E
Gb Ab N.C. Bbm Ab
got to do with it? What's love but a

Verse 2:
It may seem to you
That I'm acting confused
When you're close to me.
If I tend to look dazed,
I read it some place;
I've got cause to be.
There's a name for it,
There's a phrase that fits,
But whatever the reason,
You do it for me.

(To Chorus)

YOU ARE

Words and Music by
LIONEL RICHIE and
BRENDA HARVEY-RICHIE

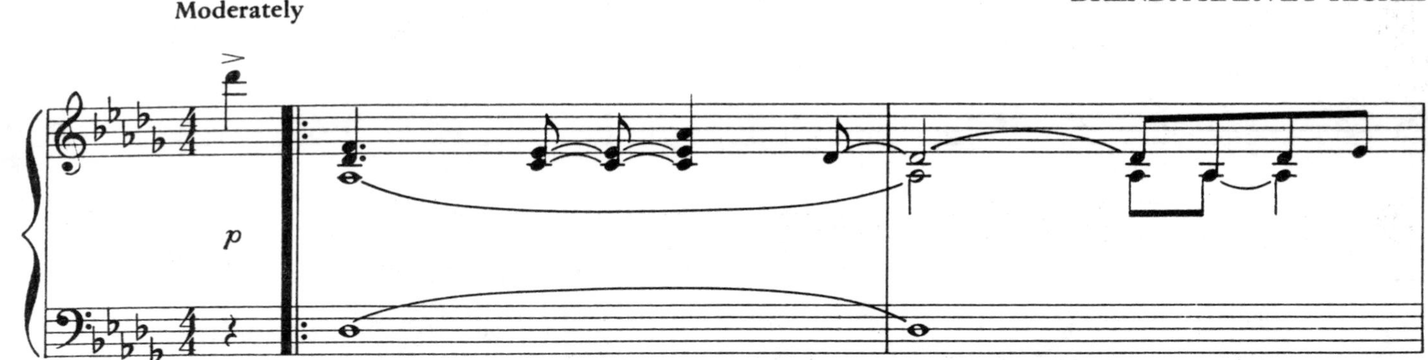

Guitar → C G/C F/C C F/C G/C C
(Capo up 1 fret)
Keyboard → D♭ A♭/D♭ G♭/D♭ D♭ G♭/D♭ A♭/D♭ D♭

Ba - by you'll find — There's on - ly one — love
Tell me it's true — I can't be - lieve — you

Am7 G/A Am
B♭m7 A♭/B♭ B♭m

Yours — and mine — I've got so — much love —
do what you do — I've got so — much love —

G
C
G/C
F/C
C
Ab
Db
Ab/Db
Gb/Db
Db
And need - ing you so My
And my love, you'll see We'll
F/C
G/C
C
Am7
G/A
Am
Gb/Db
Ab/Db
Db
Bbm7
Ab/Bb
Bbm
love for you I'll nev - er let go I've got so
stay to - geth - er, just you and me I've got so
Am/G
F
Bbm/Ab
Gb
much love All I want is to
much love On - ly you
G
C
F
Ab
Db
Gb
hold you Let me show how much I love you
(know me) Tell me how to love you

G C F
Ab Db Gb
(Show you)
(Show me)
ba - by I don't mind and I don't mind
ba - by I don't mind and I don't mind
G C F Fmaj7/G
Ab Db Gb Gbmaj7/Ab
(Lov - ing you) Girl, I love you There's no one a - bove you
(Tell me) Girl, I love you Al - ways think - ing of you
Chorus
C G/B Am Gm6 Fmaj7
Db Ab/C Bbm Abm6 Gbmaj7
You are the sun You are the rain That
F/G G C G/B Am Gm6
Gb/Ab Ab Db Ab/C Bbm Abm6
makes my life this fool - ish game You need to know I love you so

Fmaj7
G♭maj7
F/G
G♭/A♭
G
A♭
C
D♭
Am
B♭m
And I'd do it all a-gain and a-gain Oh
F
G♭
Dm7
E♭m7
Dm7/G
E♭m7/A♭
wo wo yea yea yea
1.
C
D♭
Am
B♭m
G/A
A♭/B♭
Am
B♭m
yea
C
D♭
G/C
A♭/D♭
C
D♭
Am
B♭m
G/A
A♭/B♭
Am
B♭m

2. C
Db
yea
Oh girl
F
G
C
F
G
Bb
N.C.
Gb
Ab
Db
Gb
Ab
Cb
I know you know the way I feel And I need your love for al-
Am
F
G
C
Bbm
Gb
Ab
Db
N.C.
ways 'Cause when I'm with you I fall in love A-
F
Fmaj7/G
Gb
Gbmaj7/Ab
gain and a-gain and a-gain, ba-by.

C G/B Am Gm6 Fmaj7
Db Ab/C Bbm Abm6 Gbmaj7
You are the sun You are the rain That
F/G G C G/B Am Gm6
Gb/Ab Ab Db Ab/C Bbm Abm6
makes my life this fool-ish game You need to know I love you so
Fmaj7 F/G G C Am
Gbmaj7 Gb/Ab Ab Db Bbm
And I'd do it all a-gain and a-gain Oh
F Dm7 Fmaj7/G
Gb Ebm7 Gbmaj7/Ab
Repeat and fade
wo wo

WORDS GET IN THE WAY

Words and Music by
GLORIA ESTEFAN

Chorus:
F6/9
Fmaj7
G/F
mf
words get in the way.
There's so much I want to say,
G
Dm7
C
Bb
but it's locked deep in-side, and if you look in my eyes we might
C7sus
C7
F6/9
fall in love a-gain.
I won't e-ven start to cry
Fmaj7
G/F
G
and be-fore we say good-bye.
I tried to

Verse 2:
But I know when you have something on your mind.
You've been trying to tell me for the longest time.
And before you break my heart in two,
There's something I've been trying to say to you.

(To Chorus:)

Verse 3:
Your heart has always been an open door,
But baby, I don't even know you any more.
And despite the fact it's hurting me,
I know the time has come to set you free.

(To Chorus:)

The Best Personality Folios of 1998

JIM BRICKMAN—
Visions of Love
(PF9818) Piano Solos

GARTH BROOKS—
The Limited Series
(PF9823) Piano/Vocal/Chords

DAYS OF THE NEW—
Days of the New
(0230B) Authentic GUITAR-TAB Edition

CELINE DION—
Let's Talk About Love
(PF9813) Piano/Vocal/Chords

DREAM THEATER—
Falling into Infinity
(0209B) Authentic GUITAR-TAB Edition

FLEETWOOD MAC—
The Dance
(PF9742) Piano/Vocal/Chords

FLEETWOOD MAC—
Guitar Anthology Series
(PG9717) Authentic GUITAR-TAB Edition

GREEN DAY—
Nimrod
(0224C) Authentic GUITAR-TAB Edition

JEWEL—
Spirit
(PF9836) Piano/Vocal/Chords
(PG9810) Guitar/Vocal with Tablature

KORN—
Follow the Leader
(0308B) Authentic GUITAR-TAB Edition

MADONNA—
Ray of Light
(0263B) Piano/Vocal/Chords

JIMMY PAGE & ROBERT PLANT—
Walking into Clarksdale
(6385A) Guitar/Tab/Vocal

PANTERA—
Guitar Anthology Series
(0223B) Authentic GUITAR-TAB Edition

LEANN RIMES—
You Light Up My Life: Inspirational Songs
(PF9737) Piano/Vocal/Chords

SEMISONIC—
Feeling Strangely Fine
(0284B) Authentic GUITAR-TAB Edition

SMASHING PUMPKINS—
Adore
(PG9802) Authentic GUITAR-TAB Edition

SHANIA TWAIN—
Come On Over
(PF9746) Piano/Vocal/Chords

VAN HALEN—3
(0258B) Authentic GUITAR-TAB Edition

AD 0137

BIGGEST POP HITS & COUNTRY HITS OF 1998

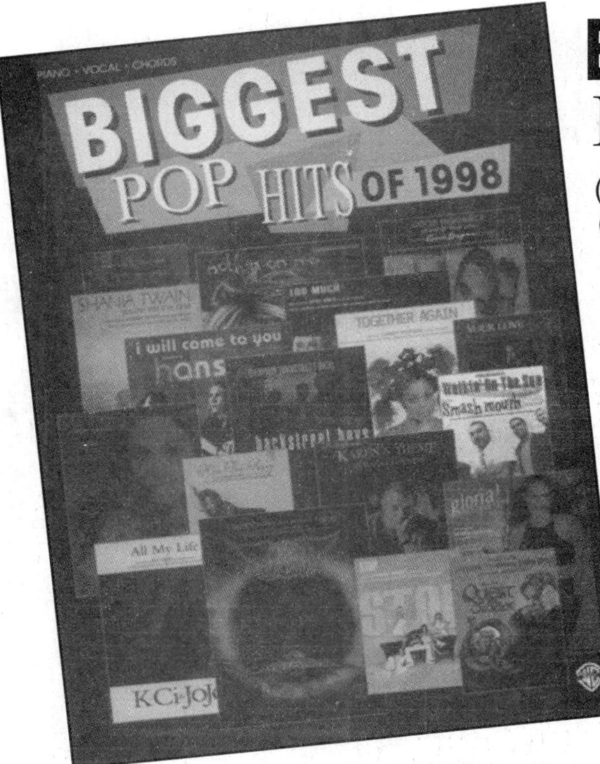

BIGGEST POP HITS OF 1998

(MF9820) Piano/Vocal/Chords
(AF9835) Easy Piano arr. Coates & Brimhall

- The biggest songs from the hottest artists
- More than 30 hit songs
- Available in P/V/C and Easy Piano Editions

Titles (and artists) include: **I Don't Want to Miss a Thing** (Aerosmith) • **My Heart Will Go On** (Celine Dion) • **How Do I Live** (LeAnn Rimes) • **You're Still the One** (Shania Twain) • **Ray of Light** (Madonna) • **All My Life** (K-Ci & Jo Jo) • **Good Riddance (Time of Your Life)** (Green Day) • **This Kiss** (Faith Hill) • **Kiss the Rain** (Billie Myers) • **Walkin' on the Sun** (Smash Mouth) and many more.

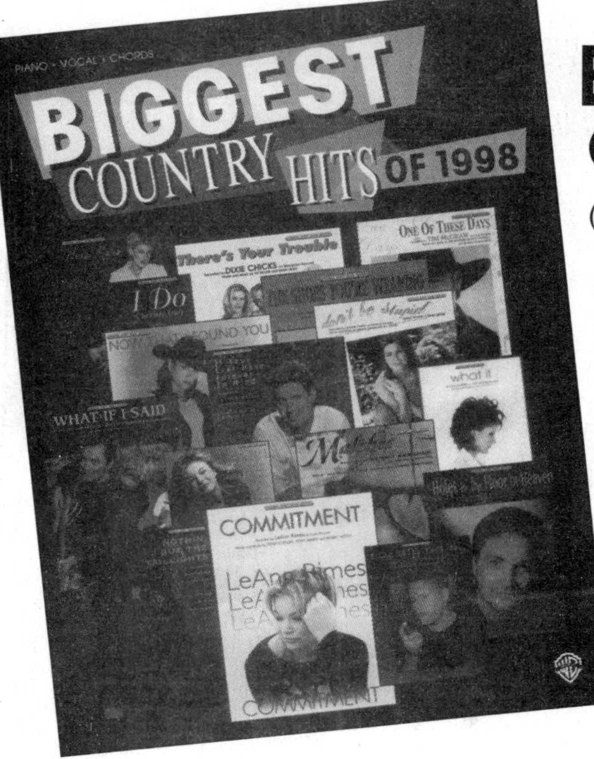

BIGGEST COUNTRY HITS OF 1998

(MF9819) Piano/Vocal/Chords

- The top country songs of the year
- The hottest country artists
- All of your favorites collected together in one great folio

Titles (and artists) include: **You're Still the One** (Shania Twain) • **This Kiss** (Faith Hill) • **Nothin' But the Taillights** (Clint Black) • **There's Your Trouble** (Dixie Chicks) • **How Do I Live** (LeAnn Rimes) • **From This Moment On** (Shania Twain & Bryan White) • **I Do (Cherish You)** (Mark Wills) • **Cover You in Kisses** (John Michael Montgomery) • **Bad Day to Let You Go** (Bryan White) • **Holes in the Floor of Heaven** (Steve Wariner) and many more.

AD 0138